The Magic of Fjord Norway

is a celebration of western Norway in words and images. By Fjord Norway we mean the four westernmost counties of Norway – Rogaland, Hordaland, Sogn og Fjordane, and Møre og Romsdal. Our aim has been to let the reader partake in a rewarding experience of the landscape and our cultural heritage.

The book is organized in themes which span from the formation of the fjords, birds and bird rocks, to the history of rain gear and modern road construction. Most of the cities are also granted a chapter.

Oil platforms and express boats are just as much a part of this book as stave churches and Viking ships.

It has been difficult to limit ourselves; there were plenty of themes to fill a book many times this size. This book is not, however, intended as just a survey of well-known tourist attractions in western Norway.

Not everything can be captured in a photograph. That is why we also look at the landscape through the eyes of painters, from J.C. Dahl to our contemporary Ørnulf Opdahl. We are invited to watch the work of a master fiddle maker and consider the landscape's influence on composers such as Edvard Grieg and Fartein Valen.

This book could not have been written without the kind help of the many experts who have shared their knowledge and insights with us. Linda Renate Campbell has made significant contributions as the co-author of a number of articles.

With a camera, we have explored western Norway, from the depths of the sea to the highest peaks – even from a bird's eye view. The last three years, each season has been spent hunting for good subjects. We have traveled more than 50 000 km and left the highways to drive the back roads as far as the last gate. Equipped with camera and plentiful supplies of film, we have enjoyed sunshine and defied storms, and had a visual feast in rain as well as moonlight.

For us, this is a never-ending journey.

– Olav Grinde og Per Eide

The Magic of
FjordNorway

Per Eide & Olav Grinde

Kom Forlag

PLACES ▶

Living Mountains

Mountains contain layer upon layer of geological history and signs. Their interpretation has become more and more refined, as geologists have learned to read the depths of the landscape that surrounds us. The history of mountains has been pushed further and further back in time.

Mount Sandsegga, Vanylven.

M ountains, too, are born, they grow and die. What has been low is raised, while the lofty is worn down. Minerals may appear from dark depths. Water, which seems one of the most yielding elements, cuts through the layers, reveals and erases.

Our mountains are still changing, albeit incomprehensibly slowly. So slow, in fact, that we don't live long enough to notice any significant changes in the landscape.

Perhaps we witness an avalanche, a boulder that breaks loose and tumbles down the mountainside before splashing into the fjord. In the course of years, we may realize that crevasses have widened, and that roots reaching into them have grown thicker. A large stone spins round and round in an eddy in the river current; we hear it groan as it gnaws at surfaces below and we understand that jagged edges are gradually smoothed out.

Books tell us that western Norway is still rising, after being freed of its immense burden after the Ice Age came to an end. That is something we can understand – we too have put aside heavy burdens.

Rivers still deposit fresh sediment on their banks. For billions of years, rivers and oceans have added new layers of clay and calcareous silt, sand and gravel. These sediments have been subjected to enormous pressures, heated to high temperatures deep within the earth, and

thus transformed into various minerals. The top layers are not necessarily the youngest. Layers have been folded and refolded, and pushed underneath older layers.

A billion years ago, Scandinavia was probably part of a vast supercontinent. 600 million years ago it split up. After the sea floor cracked, Greenland drifted away from Norway and western Europe, only to collide with them again, thus creating tall mountain ranges. Then once again, the continental plates drifted apart. Deep in the ocean, the Mid-Atlantic Ridge is still spewing out lava as it continues to crack open. In the dried lava, symmetrically on both sides, there is a magnetic record of the changing position of the poles. This ridge provides some of the most convincing evidence of the theory of continental drift.

Then 200 million years ago, the climate of Scandinavia was sub-tropical. This may have been due to the earth "twisting" in relation to its polar axis. The rich plant life of this period gave rise to thick layers of organic sediments, which were transformed into oil, gas and coal over time.

Until 50–60 million years ago, most of western Norway was a so-called peneplain, much like the rolling, relatively level terrain of today's Hardangervidda mountain plateau. The bedrock has changed little since then, although ice and water have been busy sculptors, gradually forming the dramatic landscape so familiar to many of us, and so endlessly fascinating and exotic to visitors. The fjords are very recent additions to the landscape.

Above: Panorama of Ervik, Stad.

View of Skorpa island.

The Story
of Water

Each day the sun climbs higher above the horizon. Gradually, cold winter nights turn brighter. Ice and snow retreat from the dawning rays of sun, minutely lessening the snowcaps on mountains.

The Seven Sisters are the best known falls of the Geirangerfjord.

Next page: From Gudbrandsjuvet - one of the most dramatic sections of Valldøla river in Sunnmøre.

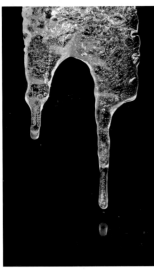

Drip drop of melting snow, trickling over the stones into a tiny beck. Rivers form. They break up the ice that has covered them, rush over clifftops, thundering against rocks hundreds of meters below – this is the farewell song of winter. Quietly, the crystal clear waters reunite, stretch their arms and follow their ancient paths toward the sea. Some of them are canyons dug deep through aeons.

The story of Norway is inseparable from the story of water. With care and fear early settlers harvested the sea. Then the Vikings mastered the waters and let the wind carry them to faraway lands.

You have to know the bleakness of winter, see it bleach the colors from the landscape, covering its hues in a mantle of white. Only then can you truly enjoy spring! Fjord Norway has few visitors during that time of year, when colors emerge from their hidden places. From one day to the next, the landscape seems renewed in delicate shades and vibrant hues. Moisture is drawn up into swelling buds, soft green leaves, unfolding flowers.

It's no secret that it rains in Fjord Norway. But when the sun breaks the cloud-cover again, and every leaf and stone and blade of grass are moist, the lush landscape seems like a million-faceted emerald.

In the sun's warm rays, children hurry to slurp in their ice cream before it melts into a white trickle. But up above, the glittering ice of the glacier retains its frozen heart. There, you can go skiing even on the hottest day in July.

Glaciers do melt, of course, releasing drops that may have been bound in ice for five thousand years. That's the best drinking water anywhere. Just bend down and dip your cupped hand into the ice cold glacier river.

Salmon rush up the rivers, even traversing waterfalls before they can mate! Kings and lords have been joined by many less noble, if no less enthusiastic fishermen. Beneath drizzle or sun, the fly-fisherman seems immersed in his own world, trying to read the river and outsmart the fish.

The mild winds and long, warm days of late summer dry out the land. Then the vibrant colors of autumn are lit. A new wind comes, less patient, whipping the coastal waters to a foaming frenzy. High waves pound the rocks, again and again. The sea throws driftwood high up on the shores and sprays its salty water onto the fields beyond; even the inland valleys quiver. But the innermost fjords remain calm and boats and gulls retreat here until the storm blows over. On a day without wind, the mirroring fjord matches the splendor of the skies. Sometimes the drizzle makes scarcely a sound. Then the hard wind returns with drenching autumn rains and hail to rip the leaves from the trees.

Suddenly one day there's frost on the ground. The tourists are gone and the birds have flown south. Distances seem to increase even though we know that's illusion.

But before the land submits to its icy sleep, before the first silent snow falls, before the sun's reflection glows one last time in the ice which creeps over the thousand lakes, and the long, drawn-out night throws its cloak of darkness over northern parts – the new spring has already sown its seeds. And these tiny seeds lie patiently under the snow, waiting. And so do we. We wait for the sun to rise once again above the horizon, wait for the sun's rays to warm the snow – for the first drip drop of melting ice.

The Ice that Sculpted the Fjords

The famous English mountaineer, William Cecil Slingsby, described Jostedalsbreen glacier as "the finest ice scenery in Europe." It's hard to disagree. Through a firsthand experience of the glacier, you may gain a deeper understanding of the massive forces of nature which carved out the fjords and the West Norwegian landscape.

Bergsetbreen looks like a wide icefall against the mountainside.

A sheet of ice up to three kilometers thick once covered most of northern Europe. It was this ice that carved out the valleys and fjords of western Norway.

As the ice flowed slowly forward in the valleys, it began carving the land. Tremendous masses of ice moved like a thick fluid under its own weight. It picked up rocks, gravel and sand and used these as abrasives to scrub the mountain clean. The powerful forces of the ice cut deep U-formed inland valleys to make lakes. But the ice kept carving, working patiently under the water surface. The last threshold was cut away and the sea came rushing in. The mouths of the fjords are much shallower than the deep fjord arms.

It has been calculated that ice carved away 5400 cubic kilometers to form the Sognefjord alone! Even so, the ice took perhaps a thousand years to carve out a humble half meter. In some places you can see the gouges and scratches made by the ice high on the mountainsides. In other places, the glaciers have deposited large quantities of gravel and rock transported by the ice.

At the Glacier Center in Jostedalen, the Norwegian Glacier Museum in Fjærland, and the Jostedalen National Park Center in Oppstryn, there are exhibitions that provide an insight into the glacier, its cultural history and the processes of Mother Nature. Exciting exhibitions tell of the life of a glacier, of how it has stretched and shrunk over the ages, and of the people who first dared explore the mighty reaches of the Jostedalsbreen.

There are many glaciers in Fjord Norway. Jostedalsbreen, which covers approximately 490 km², is the largest mainland glacier in Europe. But its beauty, which has fascinated countless travelers, is not a question of statistics. Briksdalsbreen, an arm of Jostedalsbreen, is the glacier most often seen by tourists. Other major glaciers are Folgefonna and Hardangerjøkulen in Hordaland, and Ålfotbreen in Sogn og Fjordane.

The ice of the glacier is not eternal; the oldest is "only" 5000 years old. The recent Ice Age started 70–80 000 years ago, but 6-7000 years ago the area was freed of ice. In fact, there have been at least forty Ice Ages during the last 2.5 million years. The Jostedalsbreen glacier has grown and shrunk with the changes in climate. When large volumes of snow add massive weight, faster than it can melt, the glacier's arms are pushed forward. In the last seven years, Briksdalsbreen has been lengthened by more than 500 meters.

The growth of the glacier

Jostedalsbreen is expected to grow as a result of increased snowfall over the past 15 to 20 years. The large volumes of snow form a massive weight which rolls out the glacier's arms like bread dough. In this way, the narrow and steep Bergset glacier in Jostedalen has been lengthened by several hundred meters over the last six or seven years. It now reaches the valley, pushing large boulders and forest in front of it. The long and flat glacier arms, such as the Nigard glacier, react much more slowly, and their growth is far more gradual. However, during the period of extreme cold around 1750, now referred to as the minor Ice Age, the Nigard glacier stretched 3 km in 25 years!

Each year an average of 5–6 m of snow falls on the glacier. Snow crystals are like microscopic ornaments of six-fold symmetry. Gradually these crystals are pressed into corn snow and then firn, which is more compact and contains little air. Over the years firn is compressed into dense, glacial ice.

Guided walks on the glacier

Those looking for a real challenge may take up ice-climbing. But for most of us, a few hours spent on the glacier with an experienced guide is adventurous enough. Special boots, ice-axe and crampons are provided for all, but you must bring your own clothing – remember that it is much colder up on the ice than down in the valley.

The adventurous may spend a few hours on the glacier on foot with an experienced guide. Never approach the ice without a guide – unless you want to risk a once in a lifetime experience! Deep crevasses covered in loose snow are invisible to the untrained eye. And remember that the masses of ice are constantly moving. Large blocks of ice frequently break loose from the glacial arms, so please take note of all warning signs, and do not get too close.

Explorers and scientists

Centuries before Slingsby, villagers crossed the glacier to take part in church services or weddings, drive cattle across to willing buyers, or to court available members of the opposite sex. Travelers over the Jostedalsbreen have been documented as early as the 17th century.

Briksdalsbreen - seen from within.

Around 1820, explorers and scientists began to research the many stretches of ice on the Norwegian map. Kristian Bing, from Bergen, and the Englishman William Cecil Slingsby explored the farthest reaches of the Jostedalsbreen at the end of the last century. And the guides you meet today on the glaciers are carrying on the proud traditions of Johannes Vigdal and Mikkel Mundal, who guided Slingsby on his many expeditions.

The Jostedalsbreen has grown and shrunk as the earth's climate has changed. At its thickest point, the ice is over 600 meters deep. 6000 years ago, the glacier had almost disappeared, but gradually grew back again some 4-5000 years ago. Analysis of ancient pollen found in the deeper layers of ice has provided an invaluable insight into the historic vegetation of this area.

Valleys below the glacier

Fåbergstølsgrandane, a glacial river plain in the uppermost part of Jostedalen valley, gives a good impression of what vegetation may have been like as the recent Ice Age came to an end. In this delta, there are enormous deposits of gravel, clay and other sediments. The forest lives an insecure life. While trying to cover new ground, it may be washed away as the river constantly shifts its course.

Immediately below the glaciers, hardy pioneer plants grow ever so slowly. One year they may form a rosette of leaves, only flowering the following year. One of the most beautiful of all, the arctic buttercup (*Ranunculus glacialis*), is even more careful – it may form flower buds four years before unfolding its blossoms!

The roof of the Glacier Center in Jostedal conjures two ice towers separated by a crevasse. From within the building, we stare up toward the sky from the depths of this crevasse. The beautiful building was designed by architect Rolf Sande.

Telltale signs of frost and glaciers

Glaciers leave many signs of their passing, moraines being perhaps the most obvious. Embedded in their ice, glaciers carry rocks it has broken free and grinds them with huge force against the naked bedrock. Relentless periods of frost and thaw also wear at the mountains surrounding the glacier. Ice seeps into tiny cracks and expands as it freezes, breaking loose rocks which fall onto the glacier. Some of our glaciers carry a moraine on top of the ice.

On some of the flatter summits, there are block fields formed by frost. At the foot of most mountains in western Norway there are screes that also have been formed by the changing temperatures. Some of the stone blocks may be as large as houses. When an immense section broke off mount Ramnefjell in 1905, it sent a huge flood wave across Lake Loen. A new flood wave on the 13th of September, 1936, swept a tour boat deep into the woods. Fortunately, no one was aboard for the ride!

When the glacier arms are regaining their old ground, they push earth and rock before them like bulldozers. Terminal moraines are formed where the ice stops its forward movement. By studying the various types of moraines, and which plant species have had time to establish themselves, glaciologists can read the history of a glacier. The best-known moraine in western Norway is the 500 meter long St. Olav's Serpent north of Egersund. And in the most surprising places we find impressive boulders that have been transported there by ice.

On the surface of the glacier, where slow currents of ice collide, the ice may be pressed upward into tall sculptures of transitory beauty.

In mountainsides along rivers, and in the rivercourse itself, you may see deep gouges in the naked rock. These are potholes formed by stones spun by the ice, like a drill into solid rock. After the original stone is pulverized, new stones fall into the pothole, to dig it deeper and wider when swept around by ice and water.

Glacial percussion

Near the glacier, the noise of civilization is distant, but the glacier itself is full of sound. There is a loud explosion when a section cracks off an icefall. Chunks of ice are pounded and pulverized where a glacier moves down a slope, and by a glacier river raging with meltwater, you may hear a deep rumble as large stones are rolled and shoved along the bottom.

A ride that never loses its popularity – with horse and wagon up to Briksdalsbreen.

The Soul of Fjord Norway

Thanks to our fjords, Norway has a coastline of 21 347 kilometers. That's more than the distance between the North and the South Pole! There are fjords from the Iddefjord near the Swedish border to the Kobbholmfjord near the Russian one, but nowhere are there more fjords than in western Norway.

Geologically, our fjords are very young. They have only been formed during the last two–three million years, carved by the ice that covered much of Northern Europe during a sequence of some thirty Ice Ages. When you consider that the oldest bedrock is perhaps 3.5 billion years old, that is hardly more than the twinkling of an eye!

When the ice once again retreated 10–12 000 years ago, it left behind silt and stony debris. From places that had remained free of ice, pioneer plants reclaimed the stony wasteland. Seeds carried by wind or water, or perhaps by birds, set root in narrow cracks or in powdered stone between the rocks. The grass came, flowers came – the hardiest of them. Birch and pine and willow were the first trees.

People and the land

Reindeer and other animals wandered into new pastures. Hunters followed to the rich hunting grounds. The thin soil had become fertile – settlers learned to plant seeds where they grew best. When they cast out a hook and line, they caught all the fish they could carry.

Soon the sea became source of transport as well as pantry. Some places it was hopeless to move far on foot. So people learned to build boats. Each generation improved on what they had learned and the boats became more sturdy. They set sail beyond the protected fjords, challenged the seas and sailed to foreign shores.

When the wind dies, and the fjord becomes a mirror, you may feel your boat resting on a thin membrane, with endless distances above and below. When the glowing orb of the sun touches the western horizon, the entire fjord is transformed to gold!

Music and language

Each fjord and every valley formed its own musical language. These dialects tell others where you belong, or at least where you came from.

High above fjords, you may glimpse farms, many of them abandoned. And above that again – mountain pastures. You would not believe even a goat could climb up there. But they did, and a boy or girl to watch them. Maybe that is where the folk tunes were born, melodies filled with the beauty of the land, which echoed out from the steep rock shelves, songs sung by a strong voice unaccompanied by fiddle or flute.

The fjords themselves are far from silent. Waterfalls crash down polished mountain walls and thunder is amplified as in an amphitheater. Rainfall makes every stone yield its sound, heavy drops drum against lakes and fjord. Only snow falls mutely, dampening sounds and colors. Birds migrate south, leaving Fjord Norway to the natives. In earlier times we retreated indoors to stories and crafts around the hearth, and the patient tasks of winter. Yet even in our modern times, the dark time of year turns inward on itself.

Fjords, villages and towns

They may call themselves cities – Egersund, Sandnes and Stavanger, Haugesund, Kopervik and Skudeneshavn, Leirvik, Odda and Bergen, Florø, Førde, Ålesund, Molde and Kristiansund – but not one of them is a city by international standards. The real capital of Fjord Norway is the village, tucked far into the fjord, lying in lush valleys lining the whole of the coast, or anchored to the windswept island not claimed by seabirds.

But the soul of western Norway is the fjord.

At Flydalsjuvet, one of the most photographed scenes in all of the Geirangerfjord.

Southern Fjords

Fjord Norway really begins near Stavanger, even though the Jøssingfjord is much further south in Rogaland county. The Gandsfjord, between Stavanger and Sandnes, is the most industrialized and developed fjord of all, but only along its western shores.

The dramatic Lysefjord is actually an arm of the Høgsfjord. Much of its 45 km passes between towering cliffs and mountains. Some time in the distant future, the famous Pulpit Rock will tumble into the deep fjord below; there is a deep crack toward the back of the characteristic cliff. Although spectacular, the 600 m high Pulpit Rock does not deserve all attention. The Kjerag ridge on the southern side of the fjord, which is more than a thousand meters high, is in many respects even more dramatic.

Between Stavanger and Haugesund, there is a large and complex system of fjords often labeled just Ryfylke. There are, however, fjords that are so in name only – the Kvitsøyfjord, the Hidlefjord and the Boknafjord.

The Hardangerfjord –
Blossoms Beneath the Glacier

Hardanger is never more magical than when the apple blossoms unfold at the end of May. The fruit orchards along the fjord seem to consist entirely of pale flowers, which compete in glory with the dazzling glacier and snow-topped mountains above.

Even after the flower petals have fallen, the Hardangerfjord is a feast for the eye, especially the lush northwestern shore, where the calcareous bedrock has yielded fertile soil. Between the fruit orchards are groves and woods of warmth-loving trees such as alder and linden, oak and ash, hazel and maple. Five thousand years ago, when the climate was even milder, there were great forests of such trees in Norway.

Innermost in one of the fjord arms lies the picturesque village of Ulvik. One of Norway's finest 20th century poets, Olav H. Hauge, was an apple farmer here. As you sail into the fjord and fjord arms, you pass many villages. It's hard to pick out just one to visit; they all have their own charm – Utne and Eidfjord, Strandebarm and Norheimsund, to mention a few!

Viewing the Barony in Rosendal for the first time is like rediscovering a wonderful old memory. Just as impressive are the Renaissance gardens which are used for concerts and historical plays during the summer.

Pulpit Rock - Fjord Norway's most familiar stone profile.

At the end of the 19th century Odda was the most popular cruising destination in Norway. For thousands of tourists, the great attraction was Tyssestrengene falls in nearby Tyssedalen, then the third highest falls in Europe. But when engineer Sam Eyde viewed the falls in 1906 he had a different vision, a vision of man taming these raging forces of nature and exploiting them in the

service of a new prosperity. A few years later there was a power station here and industry was established on the shores of the fjord at Odda.

Do you hear music? It may not just be birdsong. Perhaps an aspiring young musician is playing the double-stringed Hardanger fiddle, the main instrument of Norwegian folk music. One of the best instrument-makers works at the Hardanger Folk Museum, a cultural oasis in Utne. Should you be lucky enough to see a traditional wedding, be sure to study the details of the colorful costumes. A Hardanger bride is a fairytale princess – when she weds, she even wears a silver crown!

Børsheimholmen at Strandebarm,
the Hardangerfjord.

getting a stiff neck from peering up toward the tops of 1200 meter high mountains along the narrowing fjord. At Styve it's only a few hundred meters across, and near the idyllic village of Nærøy, it's not much wider. The road from Gudvangen, at the bottom of the fjord, turns into a series of hairpin bends at Stalheimskleiva. Near the hotel at the top, there is a private folk museum.

The Aurlandsfjord proper continues to Aurland and Flåm. Many fishermen have wonderful memories of salmon caught in the Aurland river – and they're not tall tales! You too will have a good story to tell after taking the train from Flåm to Myrdal, or vice versa; railway buffs consider Flåmsbana one of the most exciting train rides in all of Europe. The 20 km long railway, which passes through 20 tunnels, took 20 years to build.

Sognefjord – the Longest Fjord

The Nærøyfjord, the narrowest arm of the Sognefjord.

If the Sognefjord were drained of water, and you stood at its deepest point, you would be 1308 meters below sea level and peering up at mountains more than three kilometers high! Travelers from abroad have appreciated the scenery along Norway's longest fjord since long before the heyday of modern tourism in the middle of the 19th century. Contrary to popular belief, the Sognefjord is not the longest fjord in the world. The Nordvestfjord in Greenland is half again as long, but it is covered with ice most of the year and no one lives along its shores.

When World War I broke out, Kaiser Wilhelm II of Germany was on holiday in the village of Balestrand, visiting his friend, the painter Hans Dahl. Norwegian authorities gave the Kaiser an ultimatum to leave Norwegian territory by 6 pm that very day. Not being a man to have his pleasures cut short, Kaiser Wilhelm took his jolly good time drinking his tea, enjoying conversation with his host and savoring impressions of the surrounding landscape – before heading full steam out the fjord aboard his yacht, minutes before the deadline expired!

Balestrand, a place once favored by artists, is known for its many ornate Swiss chalet-style houses. It's just one of many charming and eye-catching villages along the 205 km long Sognefjord. Between the villages are healthy green forests, farms with rolling lush pastures, and screes where mountains have sent rocks tumbling toward the fjord.

The scenery is especially dramatic at Beitelen, where the famous Nærlandsfjord branches off from the Aurlandsfjord. There is still an old wooden quay where farmers would disembark with their sheep and head for greener grazing land in the mountains above.

For many cruise passengers, the Nærøyfjord is the climax of western Norway. There is a real danger of

If you are looking for a fine old Norwegian book, you stand a good chance of finding a real bargain, and perhaps even a first edition of the title you want in Fjærland. Hordes of book lovers from all over Norway descend on the village during the summer months. Amongst travelers, however, Fjærland is better known as the home of the Norwegian Glacier Museum. It's a perfect place to learn about the inner life of the nearby Jostedalsbreen glacier, before accompanying an experienced guide for a walk on the glacier itself.

At the end of one of the innermost arms of the Sognefjord lies the best preserved village in all of Sogn and Fjordane county – Lærdalsøyri. One of Norway's most famous salmon rivers flows right through the center of town. The oldest houses here date from the late 18th century.

Four of Norway's stave churches stand on the shores of the Sognefjord, while a fifth, Borgund, stands 27 km inland from Lærdalsøyri. The most famous of them all, and the oldest, is Urnes.

Modern engineers have drilled holes through many mountains in western Norway, even under the glacier, and have bridged many islands and fjords. But if you have to cross the Sognefjord, and want to avoid taking a ferry, you still have to drive halfway to the Swedish border.

Norwegian ponies receive a well-deserved break between heavy chores.

The Varied Landscape
of Nordfjord

The autumn and spring storms that sweep against the Norwegian coastline have Stad as their favorite meeting place. This desolate landscape, virtually devoid of trees, has a stark beauty. In the tall coastal cliffs, the relentless onslaught of the sea has carved caves both above and below the waterline. There are more shipwrecks on the sea floor here than anywhere else along the coast.

Long before roads gained their modern prominence, Selje was the most important harbor between Bergen and Trondheim. The Vikings sometimes sought shelter on this island to sit out storms which could rage for weeks. However, not everyone was patient enough to wait; some actually pulled their boats across the peninsula of Stadlandet at Dragseidet, despite a distance of 5 km and a strenuous climb up to 240 meters!

A thousand years ago, Benedictine monks from England founded a monastery on the island of Selja. The ruins of monasteries seem to disappear faster than

Killer whales in the fjords are often a sign of herring.

the wear of time would account for. It was quite common for farmers to acquire at least one stone from a holy monastery and incorporate it into the foundation of their house, so that both dwelling and family would be blessed by the Lord.

Southeast of Selje, near the mouth of the Nordfjord, lies Måløy, one of the most important fishing communities in western Norway. The old lighthouse on the island's northern tip, Kråkenes, stands in a stunning setting. At Vingen, on the southern shore of the fjord mouth, there are more petroglyphs than anywhere else in northern Europe. Just across the sound are the magnificent sea cliffs of Hornelen.

From here, the Nordfjord cuts inland, eventually branching out into a number of arms. The landscape of Nordfjord is softer than the more famous Geirangerfjord and the Sognefjord, with a lush cultural landscape and rounded mountains and hills lining the fjord.

The lakes and deep inland valleys are more dramatic; in some of them, the glacier arms of Jostedalsbreen have been making marked advances in recent years.

Don't count on sinking your fishing line to the bottom of Lake Hornindal – at 514 meters, it is the deepest in Europe. On the eastern shore is a museum dedicated to Anders Svor, a fine figurative sculptor.

There is no reason to let the season stop you if you want to go skiing or snowboarding; near the county border, not far from Videseter viewpoint, there is a summer ski center. The adventurous may spend days or even a week crossing the glacier on skis, not necessarily seeking the shortest route.

In their own humble way, Norwegians are fond of taking credit for great events. Some historians have claimed, in all seriousness, that Christopher Columbus was actually from Nordfjord, from a farming family in Hyen.

Panorama at Kvalheimsvika, Vågsøy.

The Geirangerfjord and the Golden Route

The famous Geirangerfjord does not start at the sea. It is really an arm of a greater fjord system. The Storfjord (which actually means "the great fjord") starts south of Ålesund and gradually narrows as it winds its way inland, the mountains on both sides rising ever higher. A bit past the village of Stranda, it splits into the Norddalsfjord and the Sunnylvsfjord – and it is from this latter fjord that the Geirangerfjord branches off.

A group of enthusiasts are restoring and maintaining a number of deserted farms perched on mountain ledges along the fjord, such as Knivsflå. The roaring waterfalls known as the Seven Sisters, only a couple of hundred meters away, certainly make themselves heard here. Across the fjord lies the farm of Skageflå. In days of old, young men and women supposedly courted by calling out to each other; that is a far cry from being able to whisper sweet things in the ear of your beloved!

There's a story about how Friaren became a bottle-shaped waterfall. The Suitor, as the fall may be called in English, proposed to each of the Seven Sisters. After being turned down by all of them, he was heartbroken and drowned his sorrows in drink – hence the bottle.

The Seven Sisters did not always look so impressive. In the 1930s, Ole Knivsflå took it upon himself to clean up and divide the watercourse feeding the waterfall, splitting it more clearly into seven separate falls. His motive: to create a more memorable tourist attraction!

Innermost in the fjord lies the village of Geiranger. Only 300 people live here year-round. In the winter months, it is not uncommon for them to be isolated when snow slides block the road across the mountains. In the summer, however, population figures may exceed 5000, as tourists arrive by tour bus and car, cruise ship, or ferry from Hellesylt.

From the top of Mount Dalsnibba, 1495 m, there is a fantastic view over the fjord. There is also a dramatic view from Flydalsjuvet, a stone tongue which juts out high above a river canyon, not far from the old Hotel Bellevue.

Those arriving by sea should allow time for onshore excursions. The so-called Golden Route continues by road up to Ørnesvingen viewpoint, with its magnificent panorama, before slowly descending toward the ferry quay at Eidsdal. On the other side of the Norddalsfjord lies Valldal, known for providing the juiciest, tastiest strawberries in the whole region!

Before you approach the valley of Isterdalen, you see the towering peaks known as the Bishop, the King and the Queen. They can be climbed, but only by ramblers unafraid of peering into the abyss. This is not the place to miss a step. The tempting Trollstigen trail leads to Trolltindene, the pinnacles perched above the mountain wall known to every rock climber in the world – Trollveggen.

Next page: Gjerdefossen falls.

Skrenakken, the Norddalsfjord.

Rarely has the Geirangerfjord seen so many large sailing vessels as during the 1998 Cutty Sark Tall Ships Race – and it wasn't even on the official program. Many captains were tempted to make a gratifying detour.

Our Mountain Retreats

We call it our "mountain home", a term that signals a sense of belonging for western Norwegians. Some of us need to gaze out over the ocean, others need the mountains as permanent points of reference in our lives.

Bicyclists at the peak of their adventure - Kjeragbolten, wedged 1100 m above the fjord.

A river of meltwater has carved out a cave in the deep snows of Molladalen.

It's been said that the vault of the heaven is the only true roof over the Believer. Others have maintained that when the Church tries to count its congregation, it should include most of those who seek the silence of the mountains – after all, prayer is an act of the listening heart.

A pilgrimage

During the Easter holidays, there is a mass exodus of Norwegians from towns and cities. In cars weighed down with ski equipment, sunglasses and warm sweaters, we head for the snow-covered mountains. The towns are abandoned to movie buffs and those who have to keep the wheels of civilization turning. Then, of course, there are those who fear an overdose of fresh air or are allergic to the thought of driving in the slowly winding queue which this Easter exodus often is.

In the official descriptions of Norwegian towns, mountains play a key role. Bergen is the city of seven mountains, and in the 19th century visionary citizens established Fjellvegen, "the mountain promenade". Molde prides herself on her panorama of 222 peaks. Ålesund points out the 418 steps that lead to the top of Aksla, the best place for admiring the town; Kristiansund has Kvernberget; Stavanger has Randaberg…

Any self-respecting town offers a network of well-marked trails close to the city center. Even residents of the Norwegian capital have access to wilderness a few stops away on the metro. One must wonder what long-term withdrawal symptoms which the citizens of other European cities are suffering from!

There are steep mountains throughout Fjord Norway, and for some people who live below them, avalanches are an overhanging danger. The Municipality of Odda, for instance, has used large resources and creative engineering to ensure the safety of its most exposed residents.

At the foot of many mountains we find rock debris which the frost has broken from the mountain. Gloppedalsura in Rogaland, Norway's largest scree, measures all of 1 km^2 – and some of the stone blocks are large as houses.

Pulpit Rock and Kjerag are the most famous of the dramatic mountains surrounding the Lysefjord. The mountains and hills between Lysefjord and Hunnedalen valley will soon become a national park.

Each year, the Hardangervidda mountain plateau tempts tens of thousands of ramblers. This huge national park is the home of Europe's largest herd of wild reindeer. Only the mountain lodges and peaks break the horizon of this open landscape. Southwest of Finse lies the Hardangerjøkulen glacier. Ice grips the tallest peaks nearby, too, even in the midst of summer. It wasn't always so; 5000 years ago, Stone Age hunters roamed the pine forests that grew here. Today, hunting season is restricted to a few weeks in the autumn, but Hardangervidda's many lakes and streams tempt anglers much of the year. For centuries, the farmers of western Norway have brought their sheep to mountain pastures, and Hardangervidda is one of the most popular summer grazing areas.

Before the Bergen railway was built, an annual market at Hallingskeid gathered people from Hardanger, Voss, Sogn and Hallingdal to barter and trade.

Olav Tryggvason

In his sagas, the historian Snorre writes that one of Olav Tryggvason's many feats was to climb mount Hornelen. There is little likelihood that the king was the first to enjoy the stupendous view from the top of the dark and forbidding sea cliff that marks the entry to Nordfjord. A trail from the west provides easy access.

One of the most impressive mountain regions in Sogn og Fjordane is Hurrungane in Luster and Årdal, where Store Skagastølstind rises to 2405 meters. The English mountain pioneer, William Cecil Slingsby, wrote of his memorable solo ascent in the 1880s. Norway's highest freely falling waterfall, Vettisfossen, on the eastern side of Utladalen, also must have made a deep impression on him.

Stølsheimen, on the border between Hordaland and Sogn og Fjordane, has long been a popular area for both rambling and paddling. The nearby Vikafjell mountains, where the calcareous bedrock provides for a richly varied flora, is an area still waiting to be discovered by many.

Spellbound by the mountains

But no counties have more impressive mountains than Møre og Romsdal. The most alpine formations in western Norway are Sunnmørsalpene. Trollheimen is legendary where it rises above the beautiful valley of Innerdalen, while further north, Romsdalen looks up at

Trolltindane, Vengetindane and Romsdalshorn.

It's difficult to avoid a strong sense of vertigo as you gaze more than a kilometer straight down from Trollveggen. This is paradise to climbers from all over the world who set their sights on one of the jagged peaks at the top of this cliff. But it's no sweat, really – if you wish to cheat there is a leisurely trail up the back.

Despite the similarity of names, Trollheimen lies some distance northeast of Trollveggen. Experienced Norwegian ramblers have declared the exotic Innerdalen to be the most beautiful in all of Norway.

Of course it's impossible to forget the mountains around the Geirangerfjord. Many who visit Norway become enchanted by their beauty and spend their entire holiday here. It's easy to see why the mountain area between Geiranger and Tafjord is likely to be declared a national park – lofty peaks, steep mountains plunging into the fjord, impressive waterfalls and deep river canyons provide a never-ending feast for the eye.

Magnificent mountains more than compensate for the scanty flora of Tafjordfjellene, along the fjord arm north of Geirangerfjord. On the sunny southern face of Storfjellet, however, an astonishing variety of alpines thrive in the calcareous soil.

In Sunndalsfjella, bordering Dovre national park, there are many scenic valleys, but none is more impressive than Grøvudalen. If they are lucky, observant ramblers may see tracks of wolverine and foxes, in addition to the many reindeer.

The days of summer are long in the mountain home of Fjord Norway. If you desire, you may wander for weeks from lodge to lodge with only a light backpack. The lodges not only provide comfortable beds, but also offer food supplies and perhaps even a ready meal. They are the perfect place to exchange tales around the fire, study your maps, and look forward to the first light of morning.

At such moments, especially, natives of Fjord Norway are aware of how privileged they are, and they realize how important the mountains are as their second home.

The Sunnmøre Alps with Mount Mohnstopp and "the Blade".
In the background we see Hareidlandet.

Hesjedalsfossen falls suddenly appear before you as you drive
along the eastern shore of the Indre Osterfjord.

Solitary trees sometimes catch our eye - a twisted pine weathers the storms on a promontory, a birch hangs from a cliff in defiance of gravity. Roots manage to find nutrients in cracks and crevasses, prying them open, giving the tree a firm grip on its chosen place.

The pine forests of western Norway are magnificent when tree trunks glow in the rising or setting sun. Coastal pine is not a distinct species, although their stunted and twisted form may appear very different from pines in the shielded inlands. Pines manage quite well on meager soil, where it may have little competition; they thrive on naked rock by the fjord. On the other hand, they dislike even a hint of pollution or acid rain. The coastal forests were much more extensive before farmers cleared land for grazing and cultivation. In 1999, Parliament decreed that 30 evergreen forests – most of them pine – be preserved as wilderness areas.

Stone Age hunters who left arrowheads and campsites on Hardangervidda knew a very different landscape. Five thousand years ago, much of what is now Europe's largest mountain plateau was covered with a lush pine forest.

Five to eight thousand years ago, large forests of warmth-loving trees covered extensive areas of western Norway. The climate was more humid and probably an average of 2°C warmer than today. In sheltered valleys and on the sunny northern shores of fjords, we can still see groves or small woods of oak and beech, or perhaps forests of elm and linden, interspersed with hazel, ash or alder. Near the ruins of monasteries, we may find groves of warmth-loving trees planted by monks centuries ago.

The world's northernmost freely growing beech forest grows at Seim, in Lindås north of Bergen. Near the Sognefjord and Nordfjord, there are forests of juniper that are as large as pines.

Up near the tree line, there is also a forest of sorts. But you are not likely to get lost – the dwarf birch scarcely grow taller than a man. Birch was one of the first trees to establish itself after the inland ice retreated. Pine and willow brush also arrived quite early. One of the oldest pine forests of western Norway is found at Vettismorki in Sogn og Fjordane county.

Fragrant forests, inaccessible forests

It takes time to know the forest. You have to breathe in the scents, listen to the sounds, feel the softness of moss and the roughness of rock and bark. And you must wander often enough to observe the changes between morning and evening, and the shifting seasons.

The forest floor is often a softly billowing carpet. Tufts of heather and verdant moss manage to make the impenetrable labyrinth of trees seem safe to young eyes. Worn paths are testimony that we are not the first;

A photographer needs weeks of patience and unbelievable luck in order to capture a lynx on film.

others have been here before, maybe to pick blueberries og lingonberries, or just passing through. Dew drops glow on fertile ferns – it's tempting to break off a couple to make angel wings, to soar from tuft to tuft.

Sometimes the flora appears very different only a few feet away. Sunlight pours in, the soil is deeper, or perhaps a large rock or tree shelters plants from the wind. In places the bedrock forces ground water to the surface, creating ideal conditions for plants that prefer moister soil. It may only be upon closer inspection that you discover the fantastic range of variation among the many species of moss, ferns and grass. Admittedly, some of the distinctions require the specialists trained eye for minute details.

Here and there the ferns seem to form their own miniature forest. At Ølve in Kvinnherad, there are specimens that are well over two meters tall. Ferns, by the way, are some of the world's oldest plants; 300 million years ago, they covered much of our planet.

Not all forests are meant for us to wander in. On

Fjord Norway

steeps mountainsides along the fjords or on huge screes at the foot of mountains, we see forests where there are no paths. On the western shore of the Matrefjord, for instance, there is a fascinating forest of old, twisted elm and linden trees, with alder and oak as well.

Some of the forests of Fjord Norway represent some of Europe's last ecosystems of their kind – deciduous forests as well as forests of evergreens. The reason for their primal condition is precisely their inaccessibility.

Firs and cultivated forests

In the inner valleys and along some fjords we may see forests that seem out of place – firs. Planted fir forests often have rectilinear boundaries that mark the outer limit of the tree planters' efforts. Today there are farmers and property owners that deeply regret following the advice of forestry experts to plant high-yielding forests of rapidly growing fir.

These new forests were planted by people who were in a hurry, and who didn't want to wait too long for timber and plank. That's a far cry from almost bygone traditions when trees were hand-picked for special purposes. Floors of old houses consist almost entirely of heartwood which may seem as hard as oak, whereas you can push your thumbnail deeply into panel and flooring made from today's grown-to-order trees.

There are, however, fir forests with more integrity. In the hills near Voss grows one such ancient forest. Researchers believe animals or birds must have brought pine seeds from the valley of Hallingdal, in the east. In Rindal near the border to Sør-Trøndelag county, there is also a primal forest of fir. Except for these two areas, there are only scattered patches of wild fir – in Suldal, Luster and Verma. The wild fir forest, too, is gradually gaining new ground, but the shifting winter weather of western Norway don't provide the most ideal conditions for germinating seeds.

The first fir forests were planted about 120 years ago, to provide an economic yield. The fertile soil and weather conditions of the fjord regions are so ideal, that

An old pine forest on the banks of the Rauma River.

the annual yield far exceeds the figures indicated in production tables meant for eastern Norway. This, of course, also holds true for natural pine forests here. In recent years, forestry managers have also planted many other species, including deciduous trees.

Some of the finest pine forest are those in the Kaupanger and Sogndal regions, and in Bjørkedal on Sunnmøre, an area which still maintains its ancient boat building traditions. Materials from these forests are rich in heartwood, and they have provided the very best timber and lumber for cog-built houses and stave churches, many of which are in amazingly pristine condition even after 800 years. Wood-eating insects and larvae simply don't like heartwood, which contains substances that strongly reduce the risk of rotting. That is why heartwood pine is ideal for quays, railway sleepers, ship masts, telephone poles and flag poles. Pine was also used for other purposes; in 1870, Norway produced more than a million liters of pitch and tar by burning pine. This was used to treat boats and buildings.

In the 17th and 18th centuries, great quantities of timber were exported from western Norway. The main destinations were England, Scotland and the Netherlands. Much of London and Amsterdam was built of Norwegian pine and oak, before fire regulations made brick and concrete mandatory. Demands were hardly modest when the Danish king needed new warships; a frigate might require 1200 trees. All the same – the oak forests of southern Norway were harvested far

more harshly than the western pine forests.

Year rings

When we study the cross section of a tree, the distance between year rings provides information on the changing climate, telling us which years were warm or cold, and whether the summers were long or short. A comparison of specific patterns tell us precisely when a tree was felled. So-called dendrochronological dating methods provide exact dating of old stave churches, farm buildings and boats – or, more precisely, give us the age of the materials used.

Our very own tree

It's a good tradition to let a young child plant a tree on one of its birthdays. Seventy years or so later, in fact all through life, that tree provides a very special reference and gives cause for reflection. In the courtyard of some farms and manors, there are towering trees that have stood there for generations.

Some trees have a very special symbolism. Yggdrasil was the Norse "Tree of the Universe", a gigantic evergreen ash with branches that held the stars. According to our ancient mythology, the first man and woman – Ask and Embla – were formed of wood and given the breath of life. Oak trees are a symbol of power, strength and endurance. Viking ships were often built of oak.

Many old sayings predict the weather based on the signs of trees. Few modern meteorologists, however, will confess publicly that these long-term predictions sometimes are more accurate than their own!

Treasures from the forest

Trees provide many treasures which vary according to species and season. Who hasn't felt the softness of pussy willows against their cheeks? One of the surest and most subtle signs of spring is when swelling buds of birch color entire hillsides violet, just before the tender leaves unfold. In the autumn, few trees can compete with the fiery beauty of birch and aspen.

Even after losing their leaves, rowan trees tempt birds to their branches with large clusters of red berries. Rowanberry jelly is the perfect condiment for well-prepared game. There are few places with more hazel trees than Eikesdalen in Møre og Romsdal county; but few people today have the patience to gather the great quantities of nuts that were harvested here in times past. The spiky leaves and red berries of holly make for beautiful, long-lasting Christmas decorations.

Farmers once had to cut plentiful supplies of leaves from ash trees, elm or linden to see their livestock though the winter. In order to make the harvesting easier, farmers cut off the tops of trees, so they would sprout plenty of low-lying branches.

When crops failed or the need was great, it was not uncommon for a housewife to mix finely ground elm

bark in her flour before baking. Even if the nutrient value might be questionable, you were sure to get plenty of fiber! And did you know that pine needles contain eight times as much vitamin C as oranges? Perhaps the next time you visit a café, you should insist on pine needle tea!

A stag deer.

A lush undergrowth of ferns can be found many places in Fjord Norway. 300 million years ago, they covered much of the planet.

The Birds

Sea eagle

Ornithologists, foreign and domestic, have noted that western Norway has so many small areas that seem to satisfy a surprisingly large number of bird species. On the other hand, there are few such large areas. The reason becomes clear if we look at the map, or the landscape itself. Fjord Norway consists of highly varied terrain where there may be amazing variations in microclimate. Not far from a windy promontory, for example, there may be a sheltered cove, a tranquil fjord or an island with marshlands on its leeward side that have a very rich birdlife.

At the turn of this century, there were 366 conservation areas in western Norway, 97 consisting of marshlands and 168 with habitats for sea birds. Some of the first areas to receive a modicum of protection were those near lighthouses – long before nature conservation became systematized.

A few large areas do deserve special mention, most notably Jæren. This amazingly flat coastal area south of Stavanger consists of vast cultivated fields, lakes and marshes, and beaches that extend almost as far as the eye can see. Even in the winter the climate is mild here, inviting birds to stay longer before migrating south. On the northern tip of Askøy, the island west of Bergen, lies Herdla, a nature preservation area which also draws migratory birds. On Utvær and other islands nearby, there are many sites where sea birds thrive.

The peninsula of Stad, where there is a dramatic contrast between the sandy shores and tall, imposing sea cliffs, is a meeting place of storms. But it is also unusual in other respects. In 1999, a small population of rock doves were found here, a species not seen in Norway since the end of the 19th century.

Runde, which lies west of Ålesund, is sometimes referred to as "the avian metropolis by the sea". Some 240 bird species have been observed here, more than at any other bird cliff along the Norwegian coast. Of course the birds are just as likely to be scrutinizing their human audience as well.

It is ever so slightly misleading to believe that western Norwegians are modest with respect to occupying the land. Certain types of landscape, such as large estuaries, river mouths or deltas, have no vacancies except for those bird species that can cohabitate with man. In such places, which have been irrevocably changed by development, the rich bird life of the past is gone.

Through the centuries, people have gradually transformed most of the coastal landscape. The heathlands are the result of slash and burn agriculture, as well as an overtaxation of the forests that once grew on islands and on the outermost coast. The stonechat is one bird species that makes the heathlands its home.

We have reliable 18th century observations from western Norway of the now extinct great auk. The last two birds of this species were beaten to death in Iceland.

Some bird populations have been significantly reduced. Both the red-throated and black-throated loons require lakes or freshwater areas for nesting. Temminck's stint has the mouth of rivers as its habitat. During the early 20th century, the corncrake had far better living conditions in the cultural landscape of Jæren than it does today.

Other bird species, on the other hand, seem grateful for human encroachment. Wading birds such as oyster catchers find advantage in the altered landscape. Seagulls find plentiful supplies of food at refuse sites. Other birds find high concentrations of just the insects they want near farms that keep animals. And the fulmar petrel and gannet are reestablishing themselves in western Norway.

Perhaps the most striking adaptation to human proximity is displayed by the common sparrow, a species originally from the Middle East but now common throughout the world. It lives almost exclusively near people, and often builds its nests on or near human structures. That applies to the alpine swift and the barn swallow as well, as the latter's name would indicate.

The various ecosystems are quite narrow in the east–west direction, with short distances between coastal and mountainous terrain. As a result, sea birds can be observed almost everywhere, while for example rock ptarmigans are to be found on mountainous peninsulas and islands as well.

Naturally, the Gulf Stream is a decisive factor for bird life. Due to temperate winters, Fjord Norway is the northern extent of many bird species. At the same time, Runde and northwestern Fjord Norway have conditions arctic enough to tempt the Brünnich's guillemot. The whooper swan, once almost extinct, is expanding its domain.

Successful wildlife management is yet another important factor. 20–25 years ago, there was a real danger that the sea eagle and the peregrine falcon might disappear from Norwegian skies. New laws and increased environmental awareness enabled the authorities to put a stop to the hunting of these species and the removal of their eggs.

Oyster catchers search for
tidbits in the surf.

A generation ago, many farmers were convinced that these predatory birds ate their youngest animals. A thorough 25 year study of the sea eagle, however, has not documented a single case where it has attacked lambs or other livestock. The golden eagle (sometimes called the mountain eagle) has been known to attack lamb and young goats, although much more rarely than previously presumed.

The birds have far more to fear from us – their wingless enemies. Excavations of a sea cave north of Stad, another near Ålesund, and the Vistahola cave at Jæren uncovered bones of sea birds that may not have been hunted since prehistoric times.

Today, we still hunt ptarmigan, black grouse and capercaillie, and serve them as delicacies. Three or four generations ago, it was still common to eat sea birds such as seagulls, auks and cormorants – especially eggs and young birds. Contrary to what we might expect, this was more common near towns and cities than in rural districts. The reason may simply have been better availability of firearms.

Nor is there any documentation of birds of prey killing a person, although even small birds can attack intruders with a vengeance if they feel their nests threatened. You should, however, avoid disturbing them for their own sake, too, and not just your own health!

Some owl species can be very dangerous – unfortunately, there are cases of people losing an eye. The long-tailed skua and the Arctic skua, as well as certain gulls, use a different defense tactic. If they feel their offspring threatened, they may dive at you at an unsettling 80–100 km per hour, with plenty of force to knock you

unconscious if they collide with your head. Fortunately, they usually have enough control to make sure that they don't get hurt!

Since animal populations are always subject to fluctuations, it is difficult to say exactly which changes have been caused by people. Most ornithologists avoid claiming that what we are witnessing is the result of climate changes, the greenhouse effect or global warming. Between 1950 and 1970, for instance, many southern birds drew northward, and then retreated. Statistically, it is not unusual with several years of mild winters or warm summers. Birds are some of the first animal species to adjust to such changes.

In Møre og Romsdal county, there are some lesser known areas that should be of interest to bird-lovers – the shores of northern Sunnmøre and Romsdal, and especially the unusual landscape on the islands of Smøla, which is unique also in an international context. According to the last survey, Smøla consists of 5487 islands, islets and skerries, while there are 7750 ponds and lakes. Most of these islands are flat as a pancake; a few of them have hills or crags that rise only 40 meters or so above sea level. In this terrain dominated by heathlands and wetlands, there are many species of wading birds, coastal birds, and birds that thrive in marshes.

Among ornithologists throughout the world, Smøla is known for its unusual subspecies of willow ptarmigan, a bird that elsewhere puts on a much whiter suit of feathers in the wintertime. Such a coloring would do it little good here; the snows at Smøla are usually swept to sea or melt almost immediately.

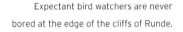

Expectant bird watchers are never bored at the edge of the cliffs of Runde.

Runde - the Avian Metropolis

It's quite a spectacle to see tens of thousands of birds flapping their wings, flying to and from their chosen spot on the 300 meter high cliffs at Runde. With marvelous precision, the airborne parents momentarily return to feed impatient offspring who seem unaffected by the dizzying heights.

No other bird cliff is visited by more species; 240 bird species have been observed at Runde. Puffin is the most numerous of them all, with 100 000 couples returning to nest. Every spring they are joined by huge colonies of kittiwake, auk, cormorants, guillemot, fulmar petrel and gannet. The cormorants prefer to nest in the large scree on the northern side of Runde, while puffins prefer the scree facing west.

On the other side of Runde, there are wetlands populated by eider duck, shelduck and oyster catchers. The island is also visited by many small birds who come here in search of food.

For bird lovers and ornithologists, Runde is paradise – no wonder it is the most visited bird cliff in all of Norway. Wildlife managers have established many good observation posts. In the summer, in order to let the birds get on with their lives, it is forbidden to stray into the nesting areas themselves.

When competition is fierce and nearby fish less than plentiful, puffins may have to fly great distances in search of food for their offspring.

Fjord Norway
- Below the Surface of the Sea

So you think that you have seen most of what Fjord Norway has to offer? Bergen and the Geirangerfjord, Pulpit Rock, the mountains of Romsdal, the myriad islands up and down the coast... But have you ever explored the underwater caves at Stad, explored old ship wrecks, admired colorful sea anemones and watched plants sway in tidal currents? And have you brought up scallops and wolffish for a feast with friends?

Amongst connoisseurs, Norway has long had a reputation as one of the world's most exciting diving paradises. In its own way, our coastal waters are just as exotic as more tropical seas. Did you know that the last World Championships in Underwater Photography of the last millennium were held outside Ålesund?

"I have dived in many seas, and many famous sites have impressed me with their beauty. Nevertheless, if I had to make a choice, I would choose the coastal waters of Fjord Norway." Per Eide knows what he's talking about. He took the photographs on these pages and those in the rest of this book; he is also four-time Nordic champion in underwater photography.

Underwater views of the fjords can be just as impressive as the famous landscape above the waterline, which is so familiar to tourists. Sheer cliffs plunge into black depths. There are caves and crevasses, screes and overhangs. The deepest fjord in the world, the Sognefjord, has depths of more than 1300 meters, near mountains almost 2000 meters high.

In the four counties of Fjord Norway, there are of course also waters with more manageable depths, sheltered by countless islands and promontories. Almost everywhere there is a fertile underwater life waiting to be explored. Near many skerries, the lush plant life may seem a submerged jungle. By the open sea, there are polished rockfaces and beaches of stones worn smooth by the surf; below the waves, there are kelp forests that hide an exciting ecosystem.

Seasons of the sea
Every season shows the diver something new. Sunny summer days bring out the glowing colors of the undersea flora and fauna. Early autumn, when there are less algae and temperatures are still mild, is an even better time to explore this silent world. In winter, colors fade and even underwater plants seem to wither. Everything looks desolate then.

"That's when I have the sea to myself. Visibility may be as much as 50 meters, and when winter light creates magical patterns in the water column, I feel as though I am a privileged witness to a secret world," says Per Eide.

In March and April, algae blossom again, providing nourishment for fish and animals that suddenly emerge from their hiding places. Colors return to the undersea world of Norway as well.

Treasure hunting
There probably still are silver and gold coins near the wreck of the Akerendam, which sank near Runde in 1725. Here, in 1974, at a depth of less than ten meters, divers brought up more than 700 kilos of precious metals. Divers are still searching for the "Castillo Negro", a Spanish ship bearing an even greater treasure, which is also supposed to have shipwrecked at Runde. Even if you don't discover gold, you may be lucky enough to see a puffin or cormorant dive for its dinner.

Hustadvika, between Molde and Kristiansund, is special for other reasons. Impressive underwater rock formations, a kelp forest, and the unusually varied fauna which includes a seal colony, have put this area on the short list for future national parks and nature reservations. There are also treasures that are out of reach of most divers. Recently, marine biologists have discovered extensive deep underwater coral reefs in Norwegian waters.

Even without diving equipment, you can get a good impression of what it's like by visiting the aquarium outside Ålesund or the one in Bergen. Another alternative,

A plumose anemone.

For a diver, it's a strange feeling to visit the foundations of the old mountain farms in Norangsdalen.

A collage of impressions from Norwegian waters.

which will keep young and old fascinated for hours, is to explore the teeming life of tidepools.

Diving to the mountain farm

"One of my favorite dives is in the magnificent Norangsdalen. In 1908, an avalanche dammed up the river. Within a week, the mountain farm and the old road between Øye and Hellesylt were submerged. It feels quite unusual to swim along the old trunk road and stone bridges, and to see the fragile remnants of trees that once grew here," says Per Eide.

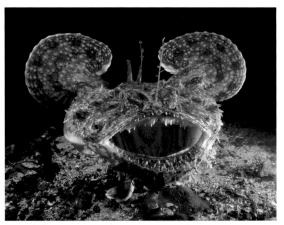

Monkfish and human anglers have something in common – they both use rod and bait to catch their dinners!

The appearance of the wolffish is just as fierce as its name. But they're surprisingly friendly fish, even allowing divers to pet them. Each wolffish is said to have its own distinct personality.

Next page: The kelp forest of Hustadvika near Strømsholmen provides excellent hunting grounds for many seals.

With a View Toward Silence

Almost everyone needs a retreat, a place for silence and reflection. For a native of western Norway, this retreat is often in the wilderness, whether in the mountains or by the sea. That's where we go for peace of mind, renewal, and to put distance between ourselves and the toss and tumble of everyday life. On Sunday mornings, many of us carry our silent prayers into the mountains and forest, rather than to church or chapel.

For city dwellers elsewhere in Europe, the wilderness is hopelessly remote. It's been centuries since anyone stood a chance of seeking peace there by fleeing these cities on foot. If you look at the towns of western Norway from a bird's eye view, however, you may be astonished at their modest demands on space. There are mountains and skerries and undeveloped land all around. A brisk ten or fifteen minute walk from the harbor in Bergen takes you beyond the last houses, and up into the green hillsides above the town, where you can ramble for dozens of miles through virtually unspoiled mountain land.

The Sunday walk is sacred to many natives. What do we seek, where do we go? To the sea where waves may wash away our worries and stress. Or to a place where the wind rustles the tree tops, a place where the color green grows and there's an emerald glow after rainfall or retreating snow, a place where autumn ignites its vibrant fires. Perhaps a place where we can stand shielded of the northern wind. A place where our thoughts may drift on patterns dancing on the water, so that we may return to our daily lives as if reborn.

We may be content to sit for hours watching a twisted pine, a huge oak with exposed roots and an arching canopy of green, an old apple tree which still bears fruit. These trees found a place to stand long before we were born, and we know in our hearts that new leaves will sprout in the spring air long after we're gone.

These are all places where we feel a sense of permanence – places where we may peer outward and inward.

Some of these secret places are inherited, so to speak. Perhaps it was here, as a child, that we felt so intensely close to our grandfather and to nature itself. As we grow older, we may bring our lover, our children or special friend here, so that we may share our secret space, a part of our soul.

Artists and philosophers often have a more acute need for spiritual concentration. After frustrating years in Oslo, with hardly any of the peace and calm needed for composing new music, Edvard Grieg found inspiration and creative rapture in Hardanger. After he and his wife Nina moved to Troldhaugen, he needed a room where he could escape from visitors and the disturbing sounds of the house; thus he had his composer's hut built by Lake Nordås, in the woods a short distance from their house.

Perhaps no other people in the world have more cabins than us Norwegians. We may not own one ourselves, but many of us have spent time at a friend's cabin. Many companies also recognize the need for a retreat, and provide cabins for their employees. Some families merely rent one as the need arises. If not, we may be moved to pack a tent and flee into the mountains. Then again, there are always the mountain lodges and hostels that everyone has come to consider their own.

A cabin shouldn't have exaggerated creature comforts. In this day and age, we may insist on running water, and we may not be willing to carry things too far from the car. But add a telephone, a nearby highway and supermarket, and perhaps satellite TV, and most Norwegians lose that good feeling of tranquil escape. A cabin should give a taste of wilderness!

Good ideas often blossom in solitude. Perhaps that is why the Norwegian philosopher Arne Næss spent altogether ten years of his life at Tvergastein, a cabin that lies 500 meters above the tree line, and a good three hour walk from Ustaoset train station. He hasn't been quite alone, however; through the years he has carried

Somehow there is always more time and space for good conversations when you're sharing a cabin with family or friends.

An evening fire at Lake Lovatn, Stryn.

up a huge library. "From here I get a proper perspective," says Næss. This is where he brought his wife on their honeymoon; fierce storms forced them to stay all of four months!

Some of us western Norwegians show withdrawal symptoms if too much time passes before we once again can peer out over the ocean. We lose our focus and an inexplicable anxiety begins to mark our face. I remember an American movie that showed a grown-up woman seeing the ocean for the first time in her life. Incomprehensible!

Seeking the edge - stormy waves and drifting snow at Hareidlandet
Left page: Seeking shelter and silence in a cave on Averøya.

The Vikings

The reputation of Vikings as plundering barbarians, who just happened to be master boatbuilders, is considerably exaggerated. By and large the Viking period saw a peaceful development, and most of the goods and treasures the Vikings brought home were acquired through honest barter.

O the other hand, there is no denying that they did carry out gruesome attacks which gave people throughout much of Europe good reason to fear them, and their violent reputations may sometimes have given them the better bargain. The attack on an unprotected monastery on the island of Lindisfarne near the Scottish border in 793 is generally considered the start of the Viking period. But history may have to be rewritten; two of the twelve ship graves that have thus far been discovered in Europe were found at Avaldsnes – and one of them, which contained a 25 meter long ship dating from 690 to 750, indicates that the Viking period began far earlier than previously believed. Surprisingly, even a Roman sword has been found at Avaldsnes!

An exodus of Norsemen

The Norsemen navigated the Rhine, sailed up the Volga through Russia, all the way to the distant shore of the Caspian Sea, before crossing to Baghdad on foot. Or they rounded the Straits of Gibraltar, visited the Mediterranean countries and reached the Middle East by sea. They acquired Arabic glass, rich treasures of coins and silver, Persian ceramics and Irish bronze. They traded away furs and honey, vessels of soapstone and even slaves.

Leif Eiriksson's discovery of Vinland – America – some 500 years before Christopher Columbus is well-documented. The Vikings also settled the Orkney and Shetland Islands, the Hebrides and the Isle of Man, Iceland and Greenland, the coast of Normandy and much of the British Isles and Ireland. In fact, Dublin was founded by the Viking chieftain Olav the White in 850. Viking ornamentation is only one indication that the Norsemen had extensive contact with the Celts and were strongly influenced by them.

The Vikings understood the key to successful marketing. When Eirik the Red returned from a huge island west of Iceland, he called it "Greenland", hoping to tempt his brethren to settle its shores.

A considerable population increase may have caused the exodus and extensive expeditions of the Vikings. But we also know that social structures were becoming more complex, giving rise to the dawn of nationhood. The sagas tell of a number of chieftains who had to flee after losing a power struggle. The sagas also tell of food conservation methods used to stock their expeditions. Some researchers believe the Vikings were the first to export prime quality Norwegian salmon – dried or smoked.

Thorough reconstructions

The restored Viking farm at Avaldsnes on Karmøy in southwestern Norway, is immensely popular with school children as well as tourists. Here, the life of the Norsemen is brought to life. All the inventory is based on archaeological finds and careful research.

A monument to the battle of Hjørungavåg.

The longhouse is modeled after the remains of a structure found at Oma in southern Rogaland. The roof looks like the overturned hull of a boat. When a strong storm toppled 30 trees on Bokkøy, the well-constructed building was left unscathed.

Insights at Forsand

There is also a very fascinating, ongoing project at Forsand near Stavanger. At various times, there have apparently been up to 15 farms at Forsand. Remains of 200 buildings have been found so far, dating from 1800 BC to 500 AD. Even though this site was abandoned before the Vikings came onto the scene, archaeological research into their immediate predecessors provides much information about their probable customs, crafts and constructions as well.

The reconstructed banquet hall at Forsand casts an interesting light on building traditions which the Vikings inherited from earlier Norsemen. The elevated roof of the central room may well have been an earlier

One of many Viking burial mounds on Gurskøya island.

Jewelry, a sword, spear and axes once used for defense - or perhaps in one of the many Viking attacks on foreign shores. Sunnmøre Museum.

stage in the development of building types such as the stave churches; and there is every reason to believe that the characteristic form of the stave churches, which often had several levels of elevated roofs, were an echo of pagan buildings of worship.

The farms of chieftains and kings

Archaeological finds on the farms of Norse chieftains provide evidence of early contacts with other countries. At Lygra in northern Hordaland, a farm which was in use more or less continually until 1350, there are foreign objects dating back to the 5th century. King Håkon the Good was buried at nearby Seim in 961 after he was mortally wounded in the Battle of Fitjar; he never reached his home at Alrekstad in Bergen. According to the sagas of Snorre, Alrekstad was used by many kings, including Harald the Fair-haired, Eiric Bloodaxe and Olav Tryggvason.

The key role of women

There were Viking tradeswomen as well as tradesmen; women had strong and in many respects equally important social roles. That only changed with the introduction of Christianity and continental ideas about new ideals for women.

Viking silversmiths made jewelry of lasting beauty. Colorful glass beads, often with sophisticated patterns, were also in great demand, as was amber. Viking women of high status were buried with incomparable treasures.

Understanding the Cosmos

The Vikings had a beautiful creation myth and their gods had quite human frailties. When they found two large pieces of wood on the shore – pieces broken off Yggdrasil, the tree of the Universe – the gods blew the first breath into Ask and Embla, the first man and woman, and bestowed them with the ability to gain knowledge.

There are many stories of Yggdrasil; the tree of the universe unites three worlds – the earth, the heavens and the underworld. A squirrel is supposedly kept busy running up and down the tree with messages between the eagle that lives in the crown of the tree and the serpent which gnaws at its roots. A suffering Odin hung in this tree willingly for three days in order to acquire the secret knowledge of the runes.

Runes, which were considered magical writing, were used to call on the gods and invoke higher powers, to honor the dead and to express ones deepest longings. Of course the runes were sometimes used for quite mundane purposes as well; in Hagia Sophia, a huge 6th century church in Istanbul, there are runes scratched into the floor indicating that "Halfdan was here!"

King Harald V and Queen Sonja onboard "Borgundknarren", a reconstruction of a Viking ship.

Ten Monasteries

The year 1030 is often referred to as the official introduction of Christianity to Norway. The rapid spread of the new religion, however, indicates that the ground must have been well prepared. There is reason to believe that Irish monks were engaged in missionary work here several centuries earlier.

There were probably strong contacts between Norway and Ireland as early as half a millennium before this. Irish legends speak of monks who set out in boats, letting God steer their course. If so, it's not unlikely that the Gulf Stream brought some of them to Norway. The Celtic monks had a much stronger emphasis on contemplation, exodus and the solitary life of prayer than their Anglo-Saxon brethren. The striking similarity between Celtic and Old Norse decorations are evidence that Irish craftsmen may have been active in western Norway. We know that the Vikings – like other pillagers and conquerors – brought back bondsmen and slaves, and they could well have been influenced by their beliefs.

A strategy for missionary

Olav the Holy, Håkon the Good and Olav Tryggvason all had monks from Glastonbury associated with their court. This monastery, located in the midst of Wessex – the only kingdom in England to keep its independence in the face of Viking conquests – seems to have laid a clear missionary strategy for the spiritual conquest of Norway. It is striking that one of these Glastonbury monks, known in Norway as Bishop Grimkjell, played a key role in spreading the rumors that led to sainthood for Olav the Holy after he fell in the battle of Stiklestad near Trondheim.

The monasteries of western Norway

Ten monasteries were built in the west of Norway in the early Middle Ages, although we don't have exact dates. Half of them were established in Bergen: Munkeliv, Nonneseter, Jon's cloister, Olav's cloister and the monastery near the old fortress. In addition, a monastery was built south of Bergen – Lysekloster.

Part of the old monastery's chapel, built by the Cistercians in the early 12th century, still stands between Bergen's bus and railway stations. Today the open, vaulted room is a memorial to those who fell in World War II. Benedictine monks built their monastery on the promontory of Nordnes during the latter half of the 12th century. Native Bergeners still refer to the area as "Klosteret" (the Monastery), even though all trace of the buildings that once stood there are long since gone. Nothing is preserved of St. John's monastery either, which was located just below today's courthouse.

The Dominicans established themselves in Bergen in 1240, just 14 years after the death of St. Francis of Assisi. We know they had a monastery near the fortress, even though archeologists have found no evidence of it. Old documents reveal a long-standing conflict between unappreciative monks and the more worldly dwellers of the area after lavatories were established on the hillside just above the monastery.

Not all monasteries were built near towns – far from it. On Halsnøy island, at the mouth of the Hardangerfjord, there are ruins of an Augustinian monastery, probably built by the chieftain Erling Skakke around 1160. On the beautiful island of Mosterøy, north of Stavanger,

stands Norway's best preserved monastery; Utstein monastery, also Augustinian, was most likely established by king Magnus Lagabøte at the end of the 13th century.

A few dozen kilometers south of Bergen, is Lyse monastery, founded in 1146 by Cistercian monks from Fountains Abbey in Yorkshire. On a tiny hill behind the beautifully situated monastery, is a grove of oak trees planted by the monks. It is also believed that monks from Lyse, who owned a large farm at Opdal in Hardanger, were the first to cultivate apple trees in Norway.

A destination for pilgrims

Two of the most important destinations for pilgrims in western Norway were the monastery on Selja, and the stave church in Røldal where the crucifix supposedly shed tears that could heal the sick. Today, Selja seems rather remote. Not so in the Middle Ages, when vessels would seek shelter on this island, which lies just south of storm-swept Stad. In fact, Selja monastery was a link between north and south.

The social role of monks

Monasteries were not just places of retreat for people who wanted to devote their lives to God and prayer. They were lighthouses of knowledge, centers of learning, and they functioned as both hospitals and retirement homes. Some noblemen and wealthy farmers gladly gave part of their earthly belongings in order to spend their last years with the monks. And when a person of stature died, a requiem was held and prayers were said for the soul of the departed. In return, the monasteries might receive large tracts of land or other costly gifts.

The monastic orders who came to Norway brought new knowledge about the medicinal use of plants, and monks and nuns eagerly did their best to care for the ill. As a result, many holy brothers and sisters died when the Plague came to Norway in 1349.

Monastic traditions abandoned

The great reformer, Martin Luther, had a traumatic experience when he tried monastic life. Perhaps these experiences help explain why Protestant churches virtually abandoned the contemplative traditions which had been a joint Christian heritage for a millennium and a half. In addition to meeting the skepticism of Protestant reformers, the Norwegian monasteries experienced a troublesome period before the Reformation. Their importance as centers of intellectual life had been supplanted by other institutions, and leaders considered the monasteries unwelcome competitor which had amassed far too much worldly wealth and power.

Most monasteries in Norway had already been closed down by the time king Christian III signed an order to disband them. Nonneseter monastery in Bergen was closed in 1528 and taken over by Vincens Lunge, a representative of the king who played a central role in the Reformation. That same year, the Dominican monastery near the fortress burned down. There were suspicions that Lunge had a hand in the fire, but this was never proved. In any case, it was striking that most of the valuable objects disappeared just before the fire.

Some of the arcade is still standing at Lysekloster monastery.

Selja - the Monastery Island

The wild and beautiful landscape of Selja gives an impression of a desolate and unspoiled island. But near the monastery lay the most important harbor between Bergen and Trondheim, and Selja played a vital role in the Christianization of Norway.

Even before the Viking Age, ships sought safety on Selja when storms raged the dreaded waters around the peninsula of Stad – "the largest graveyard in Norway". The monastery below the Sunniva cave was established by Benedictine monks in the 11th century. Despite frequent rains and storms, the monks grew herbs and grain, and kept livestock.

Boat trips to Selja

A small shuttle boat carries visitors to the island, which measures only 1.5 km^2. Those who walk about on the island often have to stop to savor impressions, not just to catch their breath. From the peak on the island center, there is a magnificent 360 degree panorama. The Stad peninsula to north seems like an arm and fist clenched in defiance in the face of the Atlantic Sea. The cave and monastery lie on the northern side of the island.

On her southern shores, the cliffs of Selja plunge into the sea. The terrain is dominated by marshes, heather, juniper and naked rock. Only a handful of people live here year-round, but wild goats feel at home on the rocky slopes of Selja and eagles guard her skies.

The Legend of Saint Sunniva

Princess Sunniva fled Ireland in order to avoid marrying a heathen king. She and her loyal followers set to sea in three boats, with neither sail, rudder nor oars. According to legend, one of the boats was shipwrecked on the island of Selja where the refuges sought shelter in the caves.

Later the locals asked Earl Håkon to remove the strangers. When Sunniva and her fellow Christians saw war ships coming, they asked God to accept their souls and have the mountain bury them.

Their last prayers were heard; the mountain collapsed, sealing the entrance to the cave.

In 996 AC, king Olav Tryggvason supposedly found the body of Sunniva still lifelike and intact, giving off the wonder odor that was a further sign of her sainthood. Just below the cave, king Olav built a church to house her relics. Later, a monastery was established nearby. To pilgrims in the Middle Ages, Selja was second only to Nidaros (now Trondheim) in importance. Some Norwegian historians have referred to the Sunniva cave as "the womb that gave birth to the new religion".

Peering down on the ruins of Selja monastery, from the cave where the intact remains of Saint Sunniva were found.

The Stave Churches

Off the beaten track, on a small headland with a beautiful view over the Lustrafjord, stands one of the world's foremost cultural memorials – Urnes Stave Church. The excellent condition of this ancient building is a fine testimony to the skilled craftsmen who built the church over 800 years ago.

Detail of the door to Urnes stave church.

Urnes is one of Norway's stave churches which has changed the least, which is one of the reasons why it is such an interesting building. Dates on the woodwork indicate that some of the building materials date back to the second half of the 11th century, although experts believe that Urnes was built around 1150. Archaeological digs around the site have proven that there was a building with underground pillars there before the church, and some of the materials may derive from the older structure.

The design of stave churches, with the elevated nave and interior with arcades and staves ending in block capitals are reminiscent of the Romanesque stone churches of continental Europe. Important traits of their architecture are probably also based on the Pre-Christian Viking style. The portals facing west and north are adorned with beautiful, deep wood carvings of intertwined animal figures which clearly stem from old Norse art and culture. There may also be a certain Celtic influence; there is a remarkable similarity to the ornamentation found in old manuscripts from Irish monasteries and church art.

Pre-fabricated stave churches

Our oldest wooden churches also bear similarity to the Viking ships built a couple of hundred years earlier. The time-honored techniques of the olden day boat builders were used to prepare the building materials for the stave churches. A common practice was to cut off the top from slow-growing pine and remove the bark from the lower part of the trunk several years before felling the tree. The wood would thus fill with sap, making it more resistant to rot. And the wooden churches were regularly treated with tar.

Even though stone was considered a more noble material, Norwegians insisted on building the vast majority of their churches in wood. It is estimated that 2000 stave churches were built during 1150-1350, an average of ten each year. About 275 stone churches were built during the same period.

The soon thousand year old church of Urnes is beautifully located near the Lustrafjord.

Hopperstad stave church.

Detail from Borgund stave church.

Carved portal, Urnes.

Aside from the building tempo, there is other evidence that the stave churches were prefabricated and the standardized parts quickly erected by specialized craftsmen. Standardized parts are based on the same unit of measurement. The use of staves, or vertically placed lumber, to build self-supporting walls was once a common construction method throughout much of northern Europe. Remnants of a 4000 year old buildings erected on underground pillars have been found in Rogaland.

In western Norway, stave churches were built by kings and chieftains, while in eastern Norway they were usually the result of a common effort by the local community. There, some of the techniques for carving decorations became part of the folk art – they are also found on several of the oldest farm buildings.

The neglect of churches

The Black Death of 1349 killed more than half of Norway's population – it took a further 250 years for the population to return to previous numbers. Many farms and villages were in fact depopulated, and the forests regained their territory. The legend of the archer who believed he heard a ghost as his arrow hit a church clock may well be based on a true story.

During the following centuries, churches were poorly maintained and very few new ones were built. As late as 1590, Jens Nielssøn, the bishop of Oslo, noted in his diary the "pitiful condition" of the stave churches. By 1650 there were 270 left, and in 1850 only 60 were still standing. Thirty years later only half that number remained. If it had not been for the renewed interest in old traditions that came as a result of the National Romantic movement, the Church Law of 1851, which stipulated that a church had to room a third of the local congregation, the rest of the stave churches might well have been torn down, too. From 1905, those 29 remaining have been protected. There are, however, artistic renderings and scale drawings of some churches long since gone. 140 portals have been entirely or partly preserved.

Stave churches still standing

There are nine stave churches in western Norway, five in the county of Sogn og Fjordane: Urnes, Borgund, Hopperstad, Undredal and Kaupanger. In 1883, Fortun stave church was moved to Fantoft in Bergen and rebuilt on private property. After it burned down in 1992, it has been painstakingly rebuilt using traditional techniques.

Borgund is considered the classic stave church. Tiers of elevated roofs end in an elegant tower, and the gables are decorated with fierce dragons. Borgund is located 30 km or so east of Lærdalsøyri, near the inner shores of the Sognefjord. There is a full-scale copy in Rapid City, South Dakota.

When the congregation wanted to tear down the stave church at Hopperstad at the end of the 19th century, it was bought and lovingly restored by the architect Peter Andreas Blix – largely at his own expense. Blix drew much of his inspiration from Borgund, which was built at the same time as Hopperstad.

Undredal stave church, 10 km northwest of Aurland is the smallest of our stave churches; the nave is less than four meters wide. The church at Kaupanger, located southeast of Sogndal, is sometimes referred to as "the stave church cathedral".

Three stave churches are located in northwestern Fjord Norway. One of them lies on the now abandoned island of Grip, 15 km west of Kristiansund. On the island of Averøy, 10 km south of the same city, lies Kvernes stave church. It has been heavily altered through the centuries and the exterior gives few hints as to its stave construction. The third church stands by the Romsdalsfjord, 15 km southeast of Molde. Rødven built in the early 13th century, has also been considerably altered. The crucifix here is probably original, while the rest of the decorations date from the 17th and 18th centuries.

As a point of curiosity, one Norwegian stave church now stands in Riesengebirge, Poland. It was given to the poor congregation of this mountain village by a Prussian prince.

Praying to be healed

Like Urnes, the stave church at Røldal lies in relatively remote surroundings, 45 km northeast of Sauda. It was one of the most important destinations for pilgrims in the Middle Ages. The main attraction then was not the church as such, but the crying crucifix. Its tears were said to possess healing powers. Crutches have in fact been found here, left behind by believers who no longer needed them.

The interior of Kvernes stave church on Averøy dates from 1630-40. Almost every inch of the walls and ceiling is decorated with traditional rose-painting. A ship decorates many Norwegian churches. It referres not only to seafaring as such, but is a symbol of the congregation's voyage of faith in this world.

Bryggen and the Hanseatic Merchants

The distinctive row of gable-end buildings glows in the evening sun, attracting proud Bergeners as well as inquisitive tourists. We won't mention names, but the surviving politicians and businessmen who lobbied hardest to have the dilapidated Bryggen torn down are now embarrassed, and are happy that they did not succeed.

Bryggen was once 300 meters long. The 58 remaining buildings represent an architectural tradition which dates back almost nine hundred years. Such wooden clusters were once a common sight in many European harbor towns.

Bryggen is a living treasure which is on UNESCO's World Heritage List. Artists and craftsmen, translators and fashion designers, architects and stone sellers now occupy the workshops and stores where Hanseatic merchants once kept dried fish and other goods. There are also cosy pubs and first-class restaurants with dangerously tilting original floors.

The narrow wood-paved passages between the long buildings invite you away from the harbor, as though to pull you deep into Bryggen's past. Bryggen was the economic center of Bergen from the time the city was founded in around 1070. From 1360, Hanseatic merchants dominated the activity of Bryggen; at times there were as many as 2000 Germans residing in Bergen, mostly involved in the export of dried fish. For centuries, services in German were held in the nearby St. Mary's Church, the oldest in Bergen, built in the early 12th century.

Seven major fires have caused much destruction. After each fire, Bryggen was rebuilt in accordance with the original pattern. The present buildings date back to 1702. In 1955, a devastating fire destroyed nearly half of the buildings. Archaeologists used the opportunity to dig down underneath the ashes, into the layers accumulated over many centuries. Bryggen is actually built on debris. The harbor waters once reached almost 150 meters further inland than today. At Bryggen's Museum at the north end of Bryggen, you can see ceramics and glass brought here from many other countries. This attests to trade links as early as the 12th century.

The great export of dried cod from Lofoten in the north of Norway, through Bergen, enriched the town or at least the Hanseatic traders of Bryggen. Those who brought the cod from northern Norway sometimes complained of being short-changed; on the other hand, the traders accused the skippers from up north of throwing water on their dried fish in order to make it heavier. One of the many tilting cranes that once lined the quay, working ceaselessly to load or unload ships, has recently been rebuilt.

From behind Bryggen, we look down on its fifth facade, a seemingly uninterrupted patchwork of slate roofs, ceramic tiles and corrugated steel. It wasn't only the smell of money and dried cod that could be "enjoyed" here. Surprising to all but appreciative locals, there is also a reconstructed herb garden, benches and beautiful rose beds tucked away in the back.

These famous facades, which date from after the rife of 1702, are much like those they replaced.

The alleyways of Bryggen beckon you deeply into its living history.

Time-Honored
Building Methods

The first inhabitants of western Norway sought shelter in caves or under rock ledges. Later, they made simple dwellings dug partway into the earth, or they made wooden framework onto which they wove branches of juniper or other trees, perhaps reinforced with clay.

Rough-hewn slate, cogged logs, and turf edged with birch bark are traditional building materials. The longhouse at Meåkneset hugs the rockface just under an overhang, which sends snow avalanches right over the rooftop. Next page: The hamlet of Havråtunet.

Like all other peoples, western Norwegians have built their dwellings of materials readily available, especially wood. Many foreign travelers who visit Norway for the first time stare in disbelief when they realize most houses are built of wood, a material so costly back home that they can only dream of something similar. While many other countries have long since decimated their forests, timber is still plentiful throughout most of Norway, not least of all in the west, where it has been a main export article since at least the 17th century.

In Nordhordland, there are still farmers who make barn walls by weaving together bundles of juniper branches. This proves excellent insulation and protects the animals against rain, while letting in plenty of air so that hay and leaves gathered for winter feed may dry.

Turf roofs have been used throughout the four western counties, and in fact, in the rest of Norway as well. It was a time-consuming task to gather the many layers of birch bark needed to protect the wooden roof underneath the turf from rotting. Today, there are specialized plastic products, but birch bark is still used for edging to honor traditional building methods.

A part of the landscape

Many old houses seem to be part of the landscape itself, while newer homes and buildings just as often give the impression that the architect has never visited the building site. The poet Rolf Jacobsen is right on the mark when he writes that our ancestors "knew the place in a way we've lost".

Building methods and old woodwork

If we inspect the houses closely, we also notice a significant difference in the quality of materials used in new and very old houses. Our predecessors chose slowly grown trees in which the growth rings are densely placed, especially for beams and floors. Some olden pine floors seem hard as oak, while your thumbnail makes a deep impression on new flooring or paneling derived from fast-grown forests.

Just try going to the lumber yard and asking this kind of wood! Or ask for an L-formed beam made of a root or branch joint grown just so. They will stare at you as if you suddenly landed on the wrong planet. Actually, it's just the times we live in that are all wrong; it would be hard to adjust the computerized saws used for mass production – even if you could find enough materials. No, the lumber dealer has to concentrate on providing run of the mill stock, not catering to the odd customer who comes through the door with strange notions of doing things the old way.

The farmers and landowners of the past knew the forests like their own living rooms. Every tree was cut down for a chosen purpose. It must have given them a sense of belonging to fell their own trees and then build their houses with the good help of neighbors and relatives. That's undeniably a far cry from leaving everything to a building contractor and materials chosen from a computerized price list.

If you study the cog joints in different towns and districts, you may notice minor variations in the cog

joint once used to build houses. Experts on the history of building methods can read signs such as this like an open book and tell you where the craftsmen came from and of which local traditions have drawn upon.

Crossing the threshold

Quite unconsciously, each of us carries out ancient rituals when we cross the threshold into another's house. It's an undeniable part of our heritage. The Norse book of wisdom, "Håvamål", provides detailed advice for both guest and host. The decorations around doors and windows indicate their strong importance. In the Viking Age, doorways were often small, so the person entering had to bend forward, making themselves quite vulnerable until fully inside. In the Middle Ages, it is mostly churches and manor houses that have wide gates and tall doors.

In our day and age, we almost take the morning sunshine pouring through our windows for granted. In the Middle Ages and before, few walls were broken, and then only by small openings. The stained glass windows in churches and cathedrals must have made a magical impression.

On the island of Karmøy, a team of experts has recreated a Viking farm, making windows of thin sheets of mica, a transparent rock. Just after it was built, archaeological discoveries in Denmark provided strong evidence that such windows actually had been used on some houses. Not many centuries ago, numerous windows were a sign of great wealth. In the latter part of the 20th century, huge panorama windows replaced those with many small panes. Decades later, some house-owners realized that doing so upset the aesthetic visions of long-dead architects. False crosspieces on windows are a poor nostalgic substitute.

Today, it's quite modern to complain about bad indoor air quality. Actually the problem is not a new invention. Heating techniques of the past weren't necessarily all that healthy. A common cause of death was "black lungs" – lungs destroyed by years of breathing smoke from fires in poorly ventilated rooms.

Solid bedrock and stone roofs

Much later, the well-to-do imported both glazed and unglazed ceramic tiles from the Netherlands, while some foreign customers requested Norwegian slate for their roofs.

Walking through the forests and pastures of western Norway, we often see the remains of foundations. Perhaps the forest has reclaimed fields once cultivated. The granite walls don't look much different from the foundations we find in Scotland, on the Shetlands or Faeroe Islands.

In the west of Norway, it's usually quite easy to build the foundation for a new house: you peel away a thin layer of earth, so you can pour concrete directly onto bedrock. In the cities, however, entire neighborhoods are built on centuries of debris. In the early Middle Ages and during the Viking Age, alleys and streets were paved with wooden planks, as they still are in the narrow alley-ways of Bryggen in Bergen. Cobblestones were quite a novelty when introduced around 1520.

Houses and buildings tell a similar story. The many tragic fires in cities and towns gradually convinced citizens and authorities that bricks and mortar might be better suited for densely placed buildings, and that fire walls made good sense.

By the sea

At many historic trading posts, there are well-kept wharf houses with gable ends jutting out over the water. Many years have passed since the last cargo of fish was loaded. And many of the workshops where boatbuilders and barrelmakers once worked long hours to keep up with demand, have been converted into homes or offices by people who have very different livelihoods. In the 19th century, large buildings were built as shelters to hang nets. Some consisted of little more than risers and rafters supporting a roof.

Some boat houses lie quite a distance from the water, while others are lifted by stone pillars or a drystone foundation to avoid damage from waves and tides.

Prosperous times

There are still places where we can see longhouses or clear evidence that they once stood there. Longhouses, in which both farming families and their animals had their assigned quarters, perhaps in addition to various storage spaces, were quite common in the rural districts, from the Middle Ages until the 19th century.

In the countryside, there are many impressive houses built in the latter half of the 19th century, some of them inspired by the so-called Swiss chalet style. The new-found economic prosperity brought new industries and livelihoods to the districts. This gave specialized craftsmen almost as good an income as their colleagues in towns and cities. In addition, the breadwinners of many families participated in the exceptionally rich herring fisheries and the rapidly expanding sea trade.

These were decades of hectic building. The Inheritance laws enacted by Parliament in 1821 and 1857 changed the landscape of the countryside in a drastic way. Many families left houses that stood in a village cluster and moved onto their own land. There are only a few of the old hamlets left – the best known are Agatunet and Havråtunet.

Some modern architecture is still inspired by the most traditional building methods. A house near Stavanger.

The church and vicarage at Eikesdal.

Old Hamlets

Today there are only a few hamlets left in western Norway. The two best known are Agatunet and Havråtunet. Both hamlets are expressions of an unbroken building tradition which dates back to the Middle Ages. To some extent, they resemble small villages on the continent.

Agatunet lies on the western shore of the Sørfjord in Hardanger. 31 buildings are preserved. Another well-preserved hamlet, Havråtunet, lies on the southern tip of Osterøy.

Agatunet.

Lesser known are Roglo, which also lies on the Sørfjord, and Isdalstunet north of Knarvik. But these hamlets have been considerably altered. In Ryfylke as well as in Sogn og Fjordane, there are remnants of other hamlets.

Havråtunet.

Stone

No building material lasts longer than stone. Hardly anywhere does the soil seem thick enough to totally cover the underlying rock. The stone of western Norway has a silent, yet complex, story to tell.

I t can hardly be said that towns and villages dominate the coastal landscape of western Norway. Quite the contrary. Seen as a whole, our human structures account for little. Most of the coastline is green and gray. During the recent Ice Age, much of Fjord Norway was scrubbed entirely clean of vegetation. Plants and trees were swept away, the soil washed into the sea. But when a warmer climate finally forced the ice to retreat, it left behind vast amounts of debris that had resulted from the slow wear and tear of ice on mountains and stone. This laid the basis for new soil. High up on mountainsides we may see chisel marks of the ice, the evidence of gnawing ice. The many moraines left behind by the retreating ice are only a few thousand years old – scarcely a moment in terms of geologic time.

Now as in the Stone Age, some of us are tempted to place stones in magical patterns, or pile one on top of the other to form lasting structures.

Breakers and storms slam against cliffs and skerries. The restless ocean continues to polish pebbles on countless shores.

Archaeologists uncover stones placed in a circle by hunters building a fire long ago. If they're lucky, they'll dig up arrowheads and tools of flint and other hard stones. Defensive walls and simple fortresses date back at least 1500 years.

A Viking woman of status might receive jewelry adorned with crystals from Hardangervidda or jasper from Bømlo from her beloved. She carried them all her life and took them with her in the grave, on her final journey. Stones were piled high on burial mounds to honor the dead. The Vikings are gone, most of their ships have returned to the earth, iron swords and spears rusted, and the fragile mica they once may have used for windows in their longhouses has disintegrated with time. But they left place names and stories in stone; the sagas mention cairns built along the coast to lead them home.

But was it the Vikings or their predecessors who started measuring the distance to their neighbor in terms of a stone's throw? Stone fences divide up the land, both cultivated fields and grazing land, reflecting a need to distinguish between "mine" and "yours". No one knows how many hours, days or years it has taken to pile stone upon stone. And these stones will lie there – this silent division of the land – long after our cities are reduced to rubble.

In the middle of fields are boulders too huge to move. Plowing lines flow around them like waves around skerries. Western Norway is not a landscape that invites straight lines!

The modern gardener, however, is grateful for a naked crag that invites hardy alpine plants. Here and there, huge stones seem placed in accordance with the

Ancient walls, such as these at Flø, provide information on earlier settlements along the western coast of Norway.

Weathered boathouses at Fonnaland, Kvam.

Not all stones can be cleared from the fields! Grateful sheep find shade by a boulder at Vefoss in Sandveddalen valley.

deep understanding of the landscape one would expect from a Zen master – or is it the hand of nature in her rock garden?

In Nordhordland and outer Sogn, it was long tradition to build the exposed southern or western wall of a house in stone. Only skillfully piled stone – no mortar!

Storehouses were almost always placed on flat stones resting on pillars, so that rodents would have no access. Just to be on the safe side, the builders left out the last step or two that would lead up to the door.

Strangely enough, there is a lack of good building stone many places in Norway. We have little of the limestone or sandstone the builders of churches and castles used on continental Europe. But we did find good soapstone, which was ideal for corners and doorways, windows and ornamented columns – and for millstones and food vessels which for exported for centuries. If the owner was wealthy, the outer walls of a building were carefully dressed with thin soapstone. Soapstone was wonderful for carving. On St. Mary's church in Bergen, started in 1130, the stonemasons signed their work, as they did on Moster church, begun 20 years later. Others, too, were tempted; the first graffiti in Norwegian churches was written in runes!

Just like the Romans, monks crushed marble and burned lime in order to make mortar to bind stones in place. Structures of this world, too, should be eternal – at least if they were built to honor God! Of the 2000 stave churches built in the Middle Ages, only 28 remain, while over half of the 270 stone churches from the same period are still standing.

Many houses and mountain farms have been abandoned through the years, but by and large, the foundations remain intact. Those who trace their ancestry are grateful that it takes such a long time for the wind and weather to erase names from gravestones. On the other hand, we might wonder where the walls of monasteries and old churches have gone. These walls have diminished faster than the elements would account for. In fact, generations of farmers and fishermen have secured a stone or ten from sacred ground in order to ensure the Lord's blessing over their own homes.

As early as 1320, Bishop Audfinn of Bergen sought men who mastered "the art of breaking slate from the mountain". It was only centuries later that slate roofs became common in Sunnhordland and Hardanger. The Church had a hand in that, too; Erik Olsen, the vicar on Stord, wrote a book just as zealous as a sermon, admonishing people to build with stone. Slate was a gift of God! It was a fine resource, a blessed building material, long lasting, and the use of slate saved time, at least in the long run.

Most of the old slate quarries have fallen silent, but thousands of houses and buildings along the fjord give testimony to good craftsmanship. Even when wooden beams fail and sag in the middle, the slate roof may remain intact.

In the towns, streets were paved with cobblestone to reduce mud and slush. They provided a solid footing for pedestrians and horses alike, so it is not so strange that citizens were obligated to pave the street in front of their houses. As early as 1707, Bergen hired an inspector to control the quality of this work. In recent years, the city of Bergen has shown new willingness to rehabilitate the -cobblestone to its honored place below our feet. Unfortunately, too few are initiated into the select company of cobblestone-layers, but recruitment is slowly increasing their numbers. And why not? Cobblestones last forever; even after centuries, they show no wear except a smoother face, a rounder edge.

Bygone generations of farmers laid down paths of roughly cut slate between the houses of their hamlets. To cross a mountain, steps were patiently cut or stepping stones firmly laid, larger stones spanned creeks, arched bridges crossed river rapids. When automobiles replaced horse-drawn carts and migrant workers prepared the way for railroads, the engineers polished their art – but the principles and stones remained the same.

Though they may look like gravestones of traffic victims, guard stones along hairpin bends have kept many drivers and passengers from toppling over the precipice. Retaining walls still support the roads when torrential rains threaten to wash away all soil. Few meters of road have been built in Fjord Norway without great efforts and sweat. Builders have had to cut into hard mountains, dig up earth and rock where there was too much of it, and fill it in where there was too little. How they must have envied their colleagues in some countries, where they could just draw a straight line, lay a foundation and pave the roads!

At last, modern road engineers are abandoning their misunderstood faithfulness to asphalt and reinforced concrete. Once again retaining walls are being properly built of stone, tunnel entrances are being lined with stone, and rest areas are often adorned with large stones placed between the planted bushes. Show me the pedestrian who prefers sidewalks of cracked cement to those of real stone!

Wet cobblestones – a familiar part of the city landscape to all Bergeners.

A barn wall at Havråtunet with piled stone and slate standing on edge, beneath woven juniper branches.

Boat Building
- Our Viking Heritage

Ever since the Vikings set sail in their longboats, Norway has been justly famous for the excellent craftsmanship of its boatbuilders. Archaeological finds indicate that the tradition is far older than the Vikings, although they refined boat building to an art. Norwegian boat builders of today continue and improve on traditions that are more than a thousand years old.

The secrets of boatbuilding have been handed down through generations for more than a thousand years. Sigurd Bjørkedal and his three sons in the process of building a copy of the Gokstad ship.

The Viking sagas describe boatbuilding as a specialized craft and tell the story of one its masters, Torberg Skavhogg, who built a 40 meter ship for king Olav Tryggvason. The only form of insurance against rough seas in those days was a sturdy boat.

From tales of ancient seafaring, historians have calculated that the Viking vessels averaged 7 knots on their longer journeys. In more recent times, Ragnar Thorseth has built copies of these Viking ships and proved their seaworthiness. In 1893 Magnus Andersen set sail for America onboard a copy of the Gokstad ship. On days of good weather he reached speeds of 11 knots.

The smaller rowboats that were found with the Gokstad ship bear a remarkable resemblance to the Oselvar, still being built in the district south of Bergen.

The similarity between boats found over the ages throughout Scandinavia gives reason to believe there was a long and unbroken boatbuilding tradition common to the region.

The oldest boats were discovered in marshes, where they had been sacrificed to the gods. The Hjortspring boat, built in Denmark around 300 BC is very similar to boats in some Norwegian pictographs. This boat, which had a crew of up to twenty, was paddled rather than rowed. Ancient boatbuilders sewed the boards together with gut. The oldest clincher-built boat found in Norway is the Halsnøy boat, dating from 330 AD, discovered near the outlet of the Hardangerfjord.

Hull designs and rudder fittings suggest that sails were not in use until the 8th century, almost 4000 years after the Egyptians and Mesopotamians made use of the wind. But the Norwegians caught on quickly and were soon sailing remarkably sturdy vessels far and wide.

Norwegians sailed large trade vessels during the 13th and 14th centuries, called knarr. Ragnar Thorseth has sailed far and wide on his reconstruction of this type of boat. As trade developed in the years after the Vikings, the size and number of vessels increased. But after the Black Death killed more than half the population of Norway around 1350, Norwegian waters were controlled by foreigners for many centuries.

Every year huge amounts of stockfish were loaded on board in northern Norway and exported via Bergen, where Hanseatic merchants made fortunes as middlemen for these cargoes.

In the 17th century, England restricted Norwegian sea trade through its Navigation Act, which was not lifted until 1849. Then Norwegians were curbed by a lengthy period of prohibitive Danish and then Swedish rule. But when the enterprising Norwegians could finally develop freely in the early 20th century, they built the second-largest trade fleet in the world!

A good eye for design is essential for today's traditional boatbuilders. Each board is carefully chosen, its width adjusted and adapted to other boards with the help of a broad-headed axe. This is one of the most important tools for the traditional boat builder. So is the angled plumb, which is used to check that the boards are at the correct angles in all places. The boards are carefully braced in place with sticks wedged against the ceiling and floor of the shop, giving the boat its proper form. Then holes are drilled and copper or iron rivets put into place, and a precisely shaped ribbed frame is added for strength.

Another technique is cravell building. Here, the ribs are joined first, like a skeleton, onto which the boards are fastened like a wooden skin. The completed boats are treated thoroughly with linseed oil and tar.

Norway – and particularly western Norway – has a suprisingly large number of boat types, and there are many interesting variations in local boatbuilding traditions. Each type of vessel is almost ideal for its purpose and sailing conditions. The shape of the boats is usually a good compromise, because the crew had to be able to row as well as sail them.

Surprisingly, many boats are built relatively far inland, near mature forests of slow-grown pines. Few places have a longer boatbuilding tradition than Bjørkedal in Sunnmøre. In some districts, hardwoods such as oak or birch were used for exposed or vulnerable parts. The famous Oseberg ship was built entirely of oak. Specially shaped materials were used as ribs and rowlocks,

for instance. The boatbuilders knew their forests well and could afford to wait for a tree with a desirable curved root or branch to reach its ideal size. The curvature of the grain had to be just right for rowlocks or ribs, lest they suffer from the strain of rough seas.

Preparation of materials would often start even before a tree was felled. Perhaps bark was stripped off up to the branches, or the top of the tree was cut off, so that the trunk would fill with resin. Sometimes the materials were submerged in the sea or in marshes for a year or two. Any materials showing signs of rot were discarded. The most vulnerable places on a ship, such as the end grain of ribbing, were drilled and filled with sea salt to prevent rotting.

While shipyards in western Norway are world leaders at building modern ships with entirely new techniques and materials, traditional boatbuilding is still going strong. Many old ships and boats have been restored to seaworthiness at Mellomværftet, the boatyard at Nordmøre Museum in the town of Kristiansund. Also at Norheimsund in Hardanger, there is a center for the preservation of old vessels. In addition many proud boat

owners have restored old fishing smacks, Hardanger sloops and other boats and vessels no longer being produced at modern boatyards.

An "oselver" is an elegant, practical and seaworthy boat which has changed little since Viking times.

Facing the Sea

The coastal sea route was the main thoroughfare until modern times. Whereas on land there are traces of old roads dating back to Viking times, the wake of a boat leaves no trace. Instead, there are ancient harbors and old fishing villages, trading posts and old inns, the occasional written account and the evidence of place names.

Along the coast, there are many places with quite a story to tell about a heyday long since past. A couple of centuries ago, they were important and centrally located for anyone traveling by sea. Few travelers preferred taking cumbersome hikes up and down mountains to reach their destinations, even with pack animals. It was far easier to use sails or oars. Harbors and guesthouses were established where travelers found it natural to seek shelter and rest.

There are many treasures along the coast – Sogndalsstrand, Espevær, Mosterhamn, Krosshamn, Glesvær, Kræmmerholmen and Fedje, Skjerjehamn, Rugsund, Vågsberget and Grip… And that is only mentioning a few.

Today, some of these settlements seem to be permanently asleep. Fishing villages were once established so that fishermen could be as close as possible to the fishing grounds. When engines increased the reach of vessels, the most remote and exposed villages were gradually abandoned as people moved onto the mainland or to more sheltered areas. During the rich herring fisheries of the 19th century, however, or when huge schools of cod drew close to the coast, the outermost villages were teeming with the activity of hundreds of boats and thousands of fishermen. It stands to reason that the merchants found it well worthwhile to run shops and guesthouses there.

And the wealthy businessmen from the cities found good reason to protect their economic interests. A royal decree granted well-to-do citizens of towns and cities a monopoly and actually prohibited the local people from starting such businesses. As a result, each city had its own sphere of economic interest. It was Bergeners, for instance, who controlled trade not only in

Hordaland, but in the two counties to the north as well. That is why it is not surprising that the architecture of Glesvær bears a striking resemblance to the building styles which were contemporary in Bergen.

The monopoly was finally revoked in 1842. Part of the traditional rivalry between towns and districts, not all of it good-natured, dates back to these chapters of Norwegian history.

All but a minuscule portion of Norway's gross national product is produced within a few kilometers of the coast or on the oil platforms offshore, essentially subsidizing cities like Oslo. That is why most of the villages and towns of the four counties of Fjord Norway still overlook the sea or fjord.

There are still villages and hamlets on the mainland that lack road connections with the rest of Norway, though many of them have been linked to the rest of society in the last few decades. It is only with the coming of the railway at the turn of the 20th century, and the road projects in the latter half of the same century, that we developed major inland population centers.

Most of the coastal sea route is well protected by islands and skerries. Even so, travelers who had to cross exposed waters had to wait for storms to abate; only a fool challenges the wrath of the restless sea. Vikings and coastal merchants, however, were not always so patient. Since the storms at Stad have been known to last for weeks, some of them actually pulled their boats across the mountain at Dragseidet – a climb of 240 m and a distance of 5 km. That's quite a feat! More sensible people, however, would wait at Selja, an island south of Stad, were there was a well-visited harbor and a monastery during the Middle Ages.

Who would have believed that Bud was the major trading post between Bergen and Trondheim in the 16th century?

Left page: The old trading post at Borgarøya, Sunnmøre.

Modern Travel
on the Sea

For centuries, the sea has been the highway for the people of western Norway. In many places, traveling by land was demanding or even hopeless. And even though billions have been used to vastly upgrade the road network, it will never completely replace the sea as a means of travel.

Only the worst of storms manage to stop the many express boats that shuttle people to their destinations. Passengers at Hareid hurry onward through the snow.

In the first part of the 20th century, many local steamship companies offered travel by sea. Most of them are history or have been merged with others, and by and large the slow passenger boats are gone. Today, people simply don't have the patience or the time. An excellent network of express boats, large and small, links together places on the coast. The shipyards of western Norway are world leaders in building catamarans and other types of express boats. While some vessels are built for domestic traffic, they are also much in demand as export articles.

As bridges are built, the authorities have revoked the licenses of ferry companies. They certainly are not interested in subsidizing a means of transport in direct competition with toll roads and bridges. Few people pause to reflect on the fact that it is the Directorate of Public Roads which administrates subsidies to ferries, because they are considered a part of the road network.

Bridges have the advantage of being available night and day; you don't have to set your watch according to the last entry on the evening ferry schedule. Anyone in that situation will tell you how liberating it is. Even so, many feel a sense of loss when their ferry is gone. It's more than just a means of transport. They are meeting

places over a cup of coffee, or they provide a quiet moment of reflection.

Island societies not yet blessed with a bridge by the budgetary authorities often feel they have to fight to maintain a reasonable frequency for their ferries. Even on smaller islands that are not fortunate enough to receive their share of state subsidies, there is often some industrious soul with a sturdy boat who earns a little extra income by shuttling visitors and residents back and forth.

Yes, the ferries and express boats tie much of coastal Norway together. For professional drivers, they are a respite from hours on the road; tourists, however, some-

times think of them as a cheap cruise. One of the most worthwhile ferry routes is between Hellesylt and Geiranger, on one of the wildest and most scenic Fjords in Norway. A close competitor, in this respect, is the ferry from Gudvangen, innermost in the narrow Nærøyfjord, to Kaupanger. Today, the ferry that chugs the Fjærlandsfjord, between Fjærland and Leikanger, runs only in the summer – but then there are multilingual guides to make the journey even more rewarding for foreigners. One of the smallest ferries still running goes between Urnes and Solvorn. But even this vessel seems big compared to the tiny seven car ferry that services the island of Barmen, south of Selja.

The coastal steamer, known as Hurtigruten, has a special place in the hearts of many people along the coast. To some, the familiar boat seem an indispensable part of life itself. In the summer, people come from all over the world to take the legendary cruise aboard these steamers.

Above: Ferry leaving the island of Edøy, Smøla.

Right: Hurtigruten, the coastal steamer, has provided reliable transport along the Norwegian coast since the 14th of July, 1893.

Culture

Blinking Lights
in Stormy Nights

In times past, the Vikings and other coastal dwellers would light pyres on mountaintops to warn their brethren that enemy ships were on the way. In our day and age, we take the blinking lights that provide safe passage along the coasts of our continents for granted. A sudden shift in color may warn a captain that he is headed for danger.

Along the 2650 km long Norwegian coast, there are 4200 lanterns, lights and light buoys. 208 lighthouses stand on strategic locations; incredibly, no two are alike. 110 of these were once manned. At the end of the millennium, all but 31 had been entrusted to full automation.

In 1655, the first Norwegian lighthouse was erected at Lindesnes, Norway's southernmost point. Almost 800 years earlier, the Vikings built a large cairn at Ryvarden north of Haugesund, which served as a sailing mark for many generations.

What is more surprising is that the Hanseatic tradesmen, who dominated trade in the north of Europe for centuries, did not build a single lighthouse to ensure the safety of their ships – at least not in Norway. They must have been familiar with lighthouses such as La Coruña by the Bay of Biscay, which was erected as early as 850, the oldest lighthouse in the world still in use.

The Hanseatic merchants argued about every silver coin and they were most unwilling to invest their profits in anything that did not bring immediate returns. Even during the late Middle Ages, when the Hanseatic League began its heyday, the maritime laws of Western Europe stated that passengers and crew were to be saved first, and that the rescuers had a right to part of the cargo as payment for their salvage work. Somehow, the League manage to force through that their ships and goods were excepted from such payment; not only that – they seriously meant the cargo on their ships should be saved first, then the passengers and crew!

The Phoenicians built lighthouses to provide safer passage for their ships as early as 3000 years ago. Throughout history, people with less noble intentions have lit fires in order to lure ships against rocks and cliffs, so as to plunder their cargo. In 280 B.C. the Egyptians built a 200 meter high lighthouse at Pharos. The famous lighthouse of antiquity was considered one of the seven wonders of the world.

A windswept life

At the remote lighthouses, life was often lonely and challenging, and certainly not suited for everyone's temperament. To fill the many hours, countless letters were written, poems and books of varying quality, and God knows how many models of ships. Carl Frederik Dirik, Norway's first Director of Lighthouses, noted that many lighthouse keepers took up painting "with hideous results".

One of these "Guardians of the Light" made sure that he always had plentiful company; with the help of a succession of wives, he fathered 25 children. On the islands and promontories on which the lighthouses stood, it was not unusual to keep livestock. Goats, for instance, managed perfectly well under these harsh conditions, and they provided milk for young and old.

Believe it or not, many lighthouses were self-sufficient. When the seas were calm, one could catch as much fish as anyone could stomach. On some wind-swept sites, every speck of soil was carefully dug up as soon as crops were harvested, and stored indoors so as not to be washed away by the winter storms. There were many telltale signs of powerful storms; one lighthouse keeper wrote that one night the storm was so fierce that waves broke a window high up in the tower and left herring on one of the top floors! No wonder some parents at times thought it best to secure their children with rope.

Coal was burned to light Norway's first lighthouses. After sailors for decades had complained about the "invisible" lighthouses, they started burning oil. In modern times, the light source is electric and for the most part fully automated. But even in a world where hardly any vessel sails without the Global Positioning System of navigation, which is based on satellite technology, there is still a need for lighthouses and lanterns along the coast.

Proposals to re-man more of Norway's lighthouses will probably remain just that, though an occasional stint as a lighthouse master would probably be ideal for many authors, artists and composers who require solitude and silence for their creative work. It is more likely, however, that several of the lighthouses that are now manned will see duty as guesthouses and art galleries in years to come.

Today, a greater light shines through a break in the clouds above Flåvær lighthouse on Herøy.

Svinøy lighthouse does not always stand dry when fierce waves break against the rocks.

The Cultural Landscape

The landscape formed by mankind's efforts to make ends meet, through generations and centuries, is called the cultural landscape. If you know how to read the signs, it has quite a story to tell.

The houses of Finnes lies on a green promontory, as far away as possible from the mountain and its unpredictable rock slides.

From the air, it may seem that western Norwegians have left their marks on but a fraction of the land. On closer inspection there are many signs, although the secrets of the cultural landscape remain hidden to many travelers. A true appreciation demands a slow tempo and sometimes even requires special knowledge.

The trained eye sees old hunting pits, vegetation changed by centuries of grazing near mountain farms, old burial mounds and outlines of the foundations of ancient dwellings. It makes out stone walls overgrown with moss supporting terraces of tilled land, slabs of slate leading across brooks to old elm trees with short trunks and many low branches once harvested for feed, and cotters' farms reclaimed by the forest.

Twelve thousand years ago, much of Norway was covered with ice. Only a few narrow stretches along the coast saw sunlight, and the mountain peaks tall enough to protrude through the icy wasteland. The soil of the Norwegian coast is still young and in many places very sparse and thin. Even cultivated land is often broken by rocks, boulders and crags. Here and there, groves of trees also seem like islands of the original landscape.

No one knows how many miles of rock walls divide up western Norway. For those who do want to immerse themselves, there are endless volumes of local history detailing what is known about each farm. Of course knowledge and collective memory only stretch so far back into the mists of time. Much is waiting to be discovered even for the trained eye.

Archaeologists have speculated about why they haven't found more farms and settlements from the Viking period. The simple explanation may be that many contemporary farm buildings are built right on top of the old ruins.

The heathlands

The vast and open heather-clad heathlands are not wilderness, rather they are a landscape formed by man which once stretched all the way from northern Spain to the Lofoten islands. There were once lush forests many places along the coast and on many islands that are now barren. Through the centuries before history was written, people burned many of them and planted in the ashes. Gradually, farming became more important than hunting and gathering, but most farm families still augmented their diet by fishing. The newly established Heathland Center at Lygra, north of Bergen, yields insight into this rich history.

In the fjords and valleys there are other types of cultural landscapes. Snowfall was the decisive factor, not altitude, to the type of farming endeavored. Along the entire coast, the Gulf Stream tempered the climate.

Hard-pressed resources

Today, 24 000 farms in western Norway, with 600 000 acres of cultivated land, are still tended. These numbers were considerably higher before the waves of emigration. A marked population increase at the beginning of the 19th century resulted in natural resources being hard-pressed. On the 4th of July 1825, 52 people set sail for New York from Stavanger onboard the "Restauration". Within a few decades, 800 000 Norwegians had emigrated to America, most of them from the four counties of western Norway. Today, there are supposed-

Grass is still dried the old-fashioned way on many of the farms above the Geirangerfjord, where there is a steady traffic of modern cruise ship.

ly more people of Norwegian descent on the other side of the Atlantic than in Norway itself!

New inheritance laws

Even with this mass exodus, mostly to America, dividing a farm among inheritors was complex, indeed. As generations passed, land was divided up into smaller and smaller lots, so that the property of a farming family might be a patchwork of tiny fields. In 1821 and 1857, Parliament enacted new inheritance laws that aimed to keep the farms intact and reduce the risk of conflict.

For centuries, homes and other buildings had been clustered in hamlets, and many chores had been carried out in common. In just a few decades, most of them were abandoned. Today only a few remain, such as Agatunet and Havråtunet. Instead, families built new houses on their own land. The result was the scattered farms we see throughout rural districts. The solidarity and social life was irreversibly altered.

Marking the land

The cultivated fields were not extensive, but the outfields might be large tracts of land. The farmers near the coast did not need to store so much feed for the winter, because most of their animals could graze outdoors year round. Sheep, for instance, managed just fine on the heathlands and on islands and islets.

On old farms by the fjords and in inland valleys we can still see trees once harvested for leaves. In the summer, the animals were sent to mountain pastures, in order to spare the low-lying grazing lands. Most farmsteads had two or three mountain farms and pastures, one of them often some distance from the main farm.

Most of the coastal farmers were fishermen as well, which ensured their families a varied diet. In valleys and mountains tracts, hunting added game to complement produce and meat from the farm. Even if crops failed,

people survived, whereas elsewhere in Europe that might cause a famine – the Potato Famine in Ireland cost hundreds of thousands of lives in the 1840s.

The sickle and the leaf-cutting knife

In areas where a lot of snow fell in the winter, away from the tempered coast, sickles and special knives used for harvesting leaves were essential tools. The farmers had to stock supplies of winter food for all their animals,

while on the coast only the cows and horses required such time-consuming efforts.

Burning turf and wood

When inland farmers wanted to make sure the family would stay warm in the winter, they swung the axe and pulled their saw. The farmers on the coast, however, took their shovels and simply dug up peat, which they dried for winter use. Several thousand years of clearing forests had increased the peatlands, so supplies are plentiful. In Ireland there is still commercial production of peat, while in western Norway, peat production is merely a chapter of our cultural history. Today, electricity is cheap and we can even buy firewood at the local gas station.

Sure beats our view at home, doesn't it? The deserted farm at Blomberg is one of several along the Storfjord that have been restored by local enthusiasts. In the distance we see Friaren (the Suitor) falls, which peers across the fjord to the Seven Sisters.

A Cradle of the Industrial Revolution

Whether you are standing on the banks of the fjord gazing up the steep mountainsides or perched at the edge of mountain plateau above, the landscape of Tyssedal is a constant panoramic delight. But it's not just about scenery. The area has a dramatic and compelling history: It was the site of the first major Norwegian hydropower station.

To the first foreign travelers who found their way to Tyssedal during the mid-19th century, the main attraction was the Tyssestrengene, Europe's third largest waterfall. The old tourist road from 1904 clings to the steep mountainside and provides walkers with a marvelous view of the peaceful valley and its idyllic scenery.

As engineer Sam Eyde looked out over the powerful falls in 1906, he was not gazing at the beautiful view, but towards the future – a future in which man harnessed the forces of nature. In only a few years, Eyde took the initiative to build a monumental dam and the power station in Tyssedal. These supplied power to the world's largest carbide factory in Odda.

Tyssedal power station, one of the largest and best preserved in Europe, stands as proof that industrial

Installing the pipestocks almost vertically up the mountainside is no work for amateurs!

buildings can be beautiful. The 180 meter long building has a majestic location on the banks of the Sørfjord. The turbine hall resembles a cathedral with its tall rows of columns. The building was designed by architects Thorvald Astrup and Viktor Nordan.

The Ringedal dam is a masterpiece of construction, and Norway's largest masonry dam – 520 meters long and 33 meters high of hand-cut stone. Perhaps the greatest adventure is to take the open cable car, a real roller coaster of a ride, 985 meters up the mountainside. From the top, you can take the several hour long walk to Troll Tongue, a jutting stone with a unique view out over the valley, or set off on longer hikes over the Hardangervidda mountain plateau.

The West Norwegian Industrial and Hydropower Museum tells the exciting history of hydropower and the

early industrial pioneers. The photographs of Knud Knudsen (1832-1915) provide some of the most fascinating documentation. He captured the many changes to this area, from the time when Tyssedal was a green oasis with two farms and some thirty inhabitants, until the valley took on a leading role in the Norway's industrial revolution.

Above: The Ringedal dam, of hand-cut granite, is 520 m long and 33 m high.

Right: The lights at Tyssedal power station are reflected in the fjord for the very first time. All photographs: The Knud Knudsen Collection, Norwegian Industrial and Hydropower Museum.

Journeying
Along Old Roads

The coastal sea route has played an unusually important role in Norwegian commerce and communications, even in modern times. Both the Gulating Laws from 950 AD and Magnus Lagabøte's Laws from 1274 have very specific regulations on the construction and maintenance of roads. But a major expansion of the Norwegian road network did not take place until the mid 19th century.

The royal route to Bergen

The road across the Filefjell mountains was probably the most important link between eastern and western Norway for thousands of years. This road, which passes through a beautiful countryside, is probably one of the earliest roads in the country. Even though it was called the Royal Route, it was well-traveled by common people. Actually it was not just a domestic road, but in time the Royal Route was extended all the way to Stockholm, Helsinki and St. Petersburg.

In 1647, it became the official Postal Route between the eastern capital and western Norway. A letter from Kristiania (now Oslo) took nine days to Bergen in 1655 – in other words not much more than slightly delayed third class post today.

In 1793, the Royal Route was upgraded into a wagon trail. Old drawings and cartoons give a dramatic impression of the original road across Vindhella – it had a gradient of 1:4! Naturally, such a steep ascent was more of a challenge to travelers than many of them bargained for.

During the 18th and 19th centuries, military engineers were in charge of much of the road construction. The road linking eastern and western Norway was of strategic importance. Fifty years later, captain Henrik Christian Finne and engineer Georg Daniel Barth Johnson completed Vindhella II, a masterpiece of road engineering. This road zigzags up the mountain in hairpin turns supported by solid support walls of handcrafted stone.

A large-scale program of road construction was deemed to be a matter of national interest, not to mention national security. The Church, too, considered this important to enable transport of the tithe paid by people in villages and towns.

Stalheimskleiva

Today, the steepest section of Norway's public road network is Stalheimskleiva. Through thirteen hairpin turns, the road climbs 270 meters in less than 2 km, with a gradient as steep as 1:5. It's best to check your brakes first! Two stunning waterfalls frame the famous road at Stalheimskleiva – Stalheimsfossen has a straight fall of 126 m, while Sivlefossen has a total fall of 240 m. The same captain Finne was responsible for building Stalheimskleiva, together with Barth Johnson. Even after Stalheimskleiva was upgraded for motorized traffic in 1936, the old support walls are still doing their duty.

The forced chores of farmers.

The farmers were not always as fond of these new roads as everyone else. Not only were they ordered to partici-

Trollstigen was considered a masterpiece of road engineering when it opened in 1936.

pate in their construction – they also noticed that the tax collectors became more efficient.

Property owners were held responsible for the maintenance of the old roads, and for ensuring that representatives of the Crown and other travelers could cross rivers and streams dry-shod. If not, they risked stiff fines. They were even supposed to keep a close eye on travelers, so thieves and crooks should not wander freely. As one would expect, these burdens of responsibility were kicked down the social ladder, to common farmers and tenant farmers.

Pack roads and hairpin turns

In his sagas, Snorre mentions the road between Naustdal and Bjørkedalen in Sogn og Fjordane. For many centuries, this was the most important overland link between the Nordfjord area and Sunnmøre. In the early 19th century, a number of fine stone bridges were built along this route.

When you drive toward Molde, across Furseteidet and past Botnfjordsaura, you can see four generations of roads if you look carefully, from the old pack roads to the new road constructed in 1976.

If you drive the old Geiranger road, you might wonder why there are numerous little 1 x 1 x 1.5 m sheds. These once contained soil, which was sprinkled on the snow in the spring to make it thaw faster.

The steep Lysebotn road, which climbs up from the innermost village in the Lysefjord, counts 27 hairpin turns before reaching the top of the mountain on its way toward Sirdal. With each turn, the view of the fjord becomes more and more stunning.

Skodjestraumen bridge, 5 km north of Skodje along Rv 661, was built in 1922. Its stone arch spans 59 meters, the longest in Norway.

An old stone bridge in Valdal, along the old, disused road to Trollstigen.

The New Roads

As late as 1960, Norwegians had to apply to the authorities if they wanted to purchase a car for private use. In the reconstruction years after the war, private automobiles were not a priority for the government of Einar Gerhardsen. A parliamentary resolution later, and the sale of cars exploded, bringing on new challenges.

Sure, there were roads, many of them even had an excellent standard, but no one could claim they were linked together into an effective network. Especially in the west of Norway, their standard left much to be desired. The old dirt roads were constructed for horse and wagon, not cars and buses and heavy transport. It was more than a standing joke when people quipped that the roads here were just wide enough so that two cars going in opposite directions could not pass each other.

At the end of the 1960s, an ambitious road building project was commenced, which in a drastic way changed communications and infrastructure, especially in Norway's four western counties. The dramatic engineering efforts including tunneling through mountains and bridging many rivers and sounds.

One Norwegian tunnel made international headlines just before World War II. The road between Stamnes and Eidslandet included what was then the longest tunnel in Europe, 658 m long. In the course of the following decades, however, tunnels were built that yesterday's road engineers would not even have dreamed of. Germans are known for their efficiency. During the occupation, they expedited the new road along the Åkrafjord in order to better link the county of Rogaland and the southern area of Hordaland county. At one point, more than a thousand construction workers were busy here.

Light at the end of the tunnel

When the Haukeli tunnel opened in 1967, it was a symbol of the new age. Norway was finally becoming a motorized kingdom. The 5 km long tunnel replaced one of the mountain passes most exposed to snows and harsh winter weather.

Since the 1970s, full-profile tunnel jigs have effectively eaten their way through even the hardest mountain rock. Tunnel building has suddenly became even more affordable. The new road between Trengereid and Voss, built at the end of the 20th century, passes through more than 40 tunnels. It's not so strange, then, that some tourists grumble about having to see Fjord Norway "from the inside"!

Some tunnels are built to bypass and protect cultural monuments. In other cases, tunnels are almost a pipe inside the mountain, running parallel to the fjord – for your own protection, mind you. Some stretches of road are quite exposed to avalanches. Along the Sørfjord, for instance, you can see gaping wounds in the mountain, evidence of massive earth and rock slides. It's best to be elsewhere when they cut a murderous swath through forests and vegetation on their wild path, before tumbling into the deep waters below.

The new tunnel between Aurland and Lærdal, measuring 22 km, will be the longest in the world – at least for a while. Not all travelers, however, are fond of spending time in tunnels; at least one of ten drivers (and passengers) feel unease in tunnels. That is why three illuminated caverns are built to create an illusion of four shorter tunnels.

Longing for the mainland

The Sotra bridge is a good example of the changes a link to the mainland may bring. Since the bridge was completed in 1972, the population on the island has more than doubled, services have been expanded, property prices skyrocketed, and large new shopping centers have attracted eager Bergeners, despite howling protests from merchants in town. There's no doubt about it – modern bridges have slowed people's tendency to abandon island societies.

The ferry link between Bergen and the island of Askøy was once one of the busiest in the country, and

The Atlantic Road, which skips from island to islet between Molde and Kristiansund, is rather exposed to the meteorological whims of the sea.

one of the few that did not require subsidies. For some local people, there is little practical change, but the psychological impact of a mainland link must not be underestimated. Western Norwegians suffer from a peculiar malady, a fear of ending up on the periphery, and of being left behind by modern development. It's amazing how many remote villages, hotels and lodges are "centrally located" in their advertisements to tourists.

There are now more than 15 000 bridges in Norway, and more than a proportionate number of them in western Norway. It's really a question of topography – sooner or later you have to cross water. Never mind that merely the interest on the astronomical construction costs would have been enough to finance a free ferry, including a fine meal, for all passengers from here to eternity. The undersea tunnel to Bjorøy is proof that cost-benefit analyses are not always carried out by the road authorities. Only 400 people live on Bjorøy.

The Nordhordland bridge was a technological breakthrough. When the final section, more massive than any oil platform, was towed in place, a Japanese delegation followed the action from a helicopter. On the 22nd of September 1994, the first cars could roll across the 500 meter deep Salhusfjord, on the world's longest floating bridge.

Much of Parliament's political work consists of endless negotiations and bickering about which districts should be favored with costly bridges and tunnels. New roads tend to bring some villages into the limelight, while others end up – well, in the periphery. The hotel that earned good money on those who traveled to Røldal is long since gone, while silence has settled permanently in Markhus on the Åkrafjord.

Scenic routes

The road maps of other countries often label a few scenic routes. In Fjord Norway, there is the Hardanger Road, the Ryfylke Road, the North Sea Road, and the Atlantic Highway which skips elegantly from island to islet almost in defiance of the, at times, stormy seas between Molde and Kristiansund… Come to think of it, it's probably easier to make a list of the road sections that don't take you through beautiful, magnificent scenery!

Road engineers are still dreaming of building a coastal highway without ferry crossings, all the way from Kristiansand in (not to be confused with Kristiansund) the south of Norway to Trondheim at its center.

If adventure is what you're looking for, here is some sound advice. Choose only the roads that wind like rivers across the landscape, instead of those which seem drawn with a ruler. You may be astonished that your drive also becomes a journey decades back in time. The outermost thoroughfare, if you want to call it that, will snail past scattered houses, across stone bridges and past wooden boats, across mountain passes that have long since been replaced by swift tunnels, and chug you out to islands where a few dozen recalcitrant locals still insist on living year round.

The old road across the Strynefjell mountains is worth a special mention, and the road along the Masfjord, the one past Gulen, and the road to Bremangerlandet – a true, hidden jewel.

You are hereby warned! While new roads speed you to your destination, on this old network of roads, one wonderful detour is likely to follow another. Or you may end up at an abandoned ferry quay with nothing but the gorgeous view.

The road past Gloppedalsura, the largest scree in Northern Europe.

Bicycle paths and picnic areas

Aesthetics are once again taken into consideration when roads are being planned. New roads should best follow the terrain, cuts and fillings not be brutal, and the natural landscape recreated with native or well-chosen plants. Some of the main approaches to the towns of western Norway resemble long, flowering parks.

Something else that's become important, although not exactly at the initiative of the road engineers, is paths for bicyclists and pedestrians. There are many places where you can bicycle for many miles without having to compete with armored traffic.

Dry-passage beneath the sea

Road developers have even dared to drill their holes beneath the sea! One such impressive tunnel is Rennfast north of Stavanger, which reaches 223 m below sea level before emerging on the island of Rennesøy. Rennfast is one of the few major projects in recent times which has been completed under budget.

An undersea tunnel links Ålesund with the airport on Vigra. For Kristiansund, a city built on islands, a sea-floor tunnel is an integral element of its link to the mainland.

Paying for the roads

Tolls remind drivers that it is very costly, indeed, to build roads in the mountainous terrain of western Norway, where fjords cut deeply inland. Road builders have to cut through extremely hard stone and suspend roads on bridges that soar across sounds and fjords.

A few years ago, a cartoon showed a car driver complaining to someone who manned one of the toll booths. "Certainly this road must be paid for by now." "I am sure it is – now you're paying to help us maintain the toll collection!"

The fact that people really should have to pay to leave their towns and cities, and not to drive into them, seems to escape everyone…

The road from Geiranger to Grotlie passes Djupvass lodge, 1016 m above sea level.

The Story of the Bergen Railway

A lot of preparations had to be made before work could start on the Bergen Railway. The surveying work alone took ten years, not to mention years of preparing the political ground. Finally it received support of the majority in Parliament and its route was decided. When the rails from east and west were finally joined at Ustaoset on the 9th of October 1907, it was the culmination of an almost inconceivable toil.

As many as 2400 workers were busy in the mountains at any one time, and more than 15 000 contributed to the project. Most of them were Norwegian, many from farm families. But some Swedes, a few Finns and even Italians did their share. The actual railway work was supervised by engineers who had special training from Leipzig or Dresden.

Horses pulled or carried heavy loads year-round – supplies, tools for the workers, and stone that had been cut or blasted loose in the tunnels. In the winter, sleds were used.

Working and sleeping shifts

A complex project such as a railway involves many different tasks. Tunnels had to be dug, of course, and the rubble removed, smiths were kept busy repairing tools, and cooks worked hard to feed everyone. Snow had to be cleared, stone blocks chiseled for support walls and bridges, snow screens built, the sleepers anchored and the rails secured.

Most of the work was organized in 12 hour shifts – and not just the work. Due to lack of quarters, the workers had to share beds or sleep in shifts.

The Gravhals tunnel

Some of the most physically demanding work was in the tunnels, and especially the 5.3 km long Gravhals tunnel. Here, the stone was so hard that the tunnel specialists who came from Italy had to give up and return home. When engineers Hornemann and Strøm were placed in charge, they attacked the job systematically. During the best month, the tunnel crews progressed 15 meters. Even though they dug from both sides, the tunnel took six years to complete. Before they were done, they had used 225 tons of dynamite, 500 km of fuses and drilled all of 350 000 holes into which to stuff the dynamite! It took three or four days to transport supplies on horses to the crews working at the remote site.

They may not have had serving trolleys that offered newspapers, coffee, chocolate or packaged sandwiches in the first years of the Bergen Railway, but the food and service in the dining car was first class!

Women in the mountains

Cooking, too, was a real challenge. It wasn't just that huge quantities of food had to be prepared on time. It had to be nourishing and tasty. And cheap. Many farmers sold their sheep while they were grazing on the plateau. Not only did the cooks had to clean up, they tried to make sure that the construction workers acquired hygienic habits.

It was probably no easy task to be a woman when the vast majority of your colleagues were men. They didn't suffer from a lack of attention! Sometimes it required brute force, and more than a little curage, to turn down the advances of the most insistent men, especially when they were drunk. The best protection was to have a boy friend or be married, preferably to one of the supervisors.

Doctors, priests and the good life

The work was dangerous as well as hard. Doctors were on site to take care of the injured and sick as best they could. All in all, 62 people lost their lives while working on the Bergen Railway. There was no Health and Safety Officer or Labor Inspection in those days, so safety routines were not exactly flawless. Poor ventilation in the tunnels resulted in several workers being poisoned by fumes from the explosives.

The priests, too, had their hands full. One of them explained that his parish was 70 km long and 7 m wide! Not even work with the finances was without risk. The cashier and his companion died in a winter blizzard while transporting wages from Voss to Haugastøl.

Average wages were 5.90 crowns for a ten hour day, which was good money in those days. Some of the workers saved up to buy a farm or property. Married men often had a large flock of kids to support at home. Some bachelors were frugal, while others wanted an immediate taste of the good life.

The locomotive picks up steam as it leaves Trengereid station.

A Bicycle Adventure
on the Mountain Plateau

When most people are done with their summer holidays, Rallarvegen, an old construction road along the Bergen Railway, offers unparalleled adventures for bike riders. Here you can cycle through unspoiled scenery for days, without encountering a single car!

No reason to hurry - an adventure on the old Rallarvegen should be stretched out over several days, with time to stare up at the stars at night.

Rallarvegen can be enjoyed from the middle of July, when most of the snow on the Hardangervidda mountain plateau has melted, to September when the fires of autumn set in. This is more than an old road – it is a cultural memorial to a bygone era. Along the old construction road, there are stone bridges, old huts that once housed workers, and snow screens to prevent the wind from blowing snow onto the railway. There are also houses once used by engineers and supervisors, many of them beautifully restored. Here on the mountain plateau, archaeologists have found Stone Age settlements and animal pits dating back 8000 years.

Many bicyclists prefer to start at Finse, avoiding the slight climb from Haugastøl. From Finse, 1222 m above sea level, it's a comfortable downhill ride most of the way to Flåm. Virtually the only exception is the ascent to Fagernut, the highest point on the road, at 1350 m.

Some parts of this railway are no longer in use; replaced by straighter, more modern sections. In fact, the sounds you're most likely to hear are not the train, but a waterfall or trickling creek, or birds singing in the morning sun.

Rallarvegen appears to be part of the landscape. Moss and lichen have made their mark on hand-cut granite. Nature slowly reclaims the building materials we use. Old scaffolding, discarded sleepers and rail ties, seem to take on the common gray of neglect.

Even in July and August, winter grips the shadows, preventing occasional patches of snow from melting completely. The Hardangerjøkulen glacier juts toward the southwestern horizon. Its dazzling reflection of sunlight forces you to squint. Patches of cotton grass also look like snow. Alpine speedwell, Arctic buttercups, saxifrages, cranesbills, poppies and various species of heather add their color to the landscape.

It's not uncommon to see reindeer. If you have a watchful eye, you may spot a fox or a stoat. A ptarmigan may blend in perfectly with the background until it moves. If you look up, you may even see a mountain eagle in search of prey.

At Kleivagjelet, a gully which marks the edge of the Hardangervidda plateau, there is an impressive stone bridge with a span of 31 meters. In the pools below, a trout sometimes breaks the water to catch an insect. Char populate several of the lakes. If you pause to fish, the beauty of the surroundings guarantees you won't be disappointed. The water ouzel, or dipper, may make a furtive appearance at a stream – this little avian is Norway's national bird.

At Vatnahalsen, Rallarvegen splits in two. The most popular route is the scenic descent to Flåm, on the shores of the Aurlandsfjord. Those who choose to head for Voss must first take the train from Myrdal to Uppsete.

The bicycle ride down the Flåm valley is the climax of the journey. You may have to walk your bike down the steepest hairpin turns, giving you even more time to enjoy the view of the fertile valley.

On a bicycle, you can choose your own tempo.

A veteran train crosses
Kylling bridge.

The Rauma Railway

The Rauma railway grabs your senses from the moment you climb aboard the train at Dombås and begin to roll across the open terrain toward Bjorli. That's halfway, but this railway journey is not a question of distance. After you cross the water divide and the county border, you feel the valley of Romsdal grips you more tightly as the train hugs the mountain shelf, with the abyss and a gradually wilder landscape on your left. Suddenly you are in darkness, inside the corkscrew tunnels near Verma, which wind you down to lower levels inside the mountain, before your fate is suspended on an 80 year old arched stone bridge, you cross the valley and accelerate down to join the Rauma river, you stretch your neck to peer up at Romsdalhorn, stretching a mile higher toward heaven while the precipitous Trollveggen squeezes you from the left, and then the valley suddenly widens and releases you to the luminous fjord and the sky that stretches ahead of you at journey's end: Åndalsnes.

Not so strange that you need time to catch your breath, after ninety minutes and 114 scenic kilometers.

The Flåmsbana Rail

There is never a dull moment on the train between Myrdal and Flåm.

F ew Norwegians celebrated when the Flåmsbana rail opened on 1 August 1940, even though many workers had struggled for 20 years to build the railway link between Myrdal and Flåm. It was undeniably bitter to see that the prime purpose of this masterpiece of engineering would be to transport soldiers and materiel of the German occupation forces. Today, however, Norwegians and foreign visitors alike can properly appreciate this train ride, which passes through some of the most dramatic landscape in all of Europe.

On its 20 km journey, the Flåmsbana railway passes through 20 tunnels with gradients up to 1:18. The difference in altitude between Myrdal and Flåm is all of 865 meters. It took true courage to challenge the forbidding terrain with the tools of the time. By and large, the railway was built by hand, with chisel and hand drill, through some of the hardest stone around. More than a few engineers have come from afar to study the admirable construction techniques, not least of all the 180° tunnel just above Kjosfoss station.

When Parliament voted to build Flåmsbana, the major argument was that the rail would be beneficial for commerce and development in Sogn og Fjordane. For many decades, the village of Flåm down by the fjord was an important node for freight transport to and from the county.

Railway connoisseurs rightly consider Flåmsbana the most exciting railway ride in all of Europe. The first stretch after you leave Myrdal station may seem ordinary. The drama begins as soon as the train starts its descent down the Flåm valley. The railway line traverses deep canyons, hugs mountain shelves, speeds in and out of tunnels, passes snow-topped mountains and offers lush views of the green valley below. It's a glorious, constantly changing 40 minute panorama.

Kjosfossen falls, at which the train always stops in the summer, must be the most photographed waterfall in all of Norway. But you can get the best view of the railway by bicycling or walking the old construction road, at your own chosen pace.

Olav Vindal puts the final touches on a Hardanger fiddle before leaving it in the care of a grateful fiddler.

The Hardanger Fiddle

"The instrument maker always keeps in mind the sound that should come from a mature fiddle. A new fiddle should be a bit sharp and harsh in its sound, not too mellow." Olav Vindal knows what he is talking about. He is the fiddle maker at the Hardanger Folk Museum in Utne, Norway.

A good instrument gets better with time. Just as in a good marriage the parts learn to live together in harmony. But no one can predict whether an instrument is going to be a success. Even the famous violin and fiddle makers of the past occasionally made poor instruments.

The feel of the wood

Some years ago, a Japanese producer used data technology to make some very promising violins. Unfortunately, the beautiful sound changed to the worse as the instruments aged – the opposite of what happens with a good instrument.

"The old masters did everything by hand. I think that gave them a knowledge and feeling that is impossible to obtain in any other way." The only power tool Olav Vindal uses is a band saw with a thin blade to cut out the shape. "It's important to stay in touch with the wood; every piece is unique. That is one of the reasons an instrument can never be copied".

Spruce and maple are the materials traditionally used for the Hardanger fiddle. The lid of the body is made of spruce while maple is used for the bottom. That gives a penetrating, somewhat hard tone. Sometimes black alder is used instead of maple, giving a warmer tone. The instrument maker may have to make some of the tools himself. A special wood scraper consisting of just a flat piece of steel has been cut to the exact curvature that Vindal wants for the edge of the lid.

A good fiddle is made to last. There are Hardanger fiddles made in the 1860s that are still in use – some of today's best instruments were made between 1910 and 1940.

A lot of thought goes into each part of the fiddle. In the last hundred years, there have been minor adjustments that give the fiddle a more powerful sound. It is primarily the height of the rib that determines the volume of the music. The neck and finger board were once made of goat or sheep horn. At the end of the 19th century ebony, the same wood used for the black keys of quality pianos, was introduced.

Sunning the instrument

The old Italian masters would actually hang their newly made fiddles in the sun. This gave the instrument a beautiful patina and accelerated the early stages of the aging process. Olav Vindal uses a special ultraviolet light closet for the same purpose.

At first glance it is the intricate ornamentation that distinguishes the Hardanger fiddle from the classical violin. "I prefer to carve the peg stock and head myself. But Gudmund Kjerland, a painter known for his beautiful floral patterns, decorates the surfaces with black ink drawings."

At one time it was popular to use modern glues, both for production and repairs. But by and large, these don't really harden and thus they muffle the sound. The best glue is still the horn glue that has been used for centuries.

Always a student

For generations, experienced hands have guided younger hands. That is how all craft traditions are passed on through the ages. "You need to have a deep respect for the old masters, says Olav Vindal." He often talks to his teacher Håvard Kvandal, now 90, who

taught him the art of making fiddles. "I am still a student. There is always more to learn. You are always searching for a better sound."

Vindal has never kept a ledger, but he reckons it takes him about 200 hours to make a fiddle. "I make between six and ten fiddles a year. This one is no. 59," he says, looking inside the instrument. Each of his fiddles are numbered.

"I know others who mass produce the various parts. I make one instrument at a time. And for me it's important to work undisturbed when I am forming and gluing the body of the fiddle. I have to experience this as one continuous process."

Before silence releases the sound
"You have to be able to play, at least as an amateur, if you are going to make decent fiddles."

As the wood is gradually given its carefully balanced form, shaped into just the right lines and thickness, the master instrument maker can start to hear the sound – before silence releases it. That is the secret of the music. And that is how a true Hardanger fiddle is made.

In the sensitive hands of a master fiddle maker, the instrument passes through many stages before it makes music.

Traditional Costume
– the Bunad

The traditional costume of Norway, the "bunad", is complex and costly clothing – unless of course you are lucky enough to inherit a bunad or have chosen to spend the many hours required to make one properly.

No one knows how many models and variations there actually are of all the bunads!

Traditions are being renewed; many girls receive a bunad just prior to their confirmation. It's a costume she will treasure and wear for special occasions for many years. The floral borders of skirts, bright linen shirts, colorful bead-embellished bodices and beautifully embroidered shawls make this seem like royal garb.

There are bunads for men too, but they're not worn nearly as often. Some men do, however, don this finery when they take a bride to wed.

Norwegian peasants and farmers were considerably better off than their counterparts elsewhere in Europe. Tradition dictated that a farmer's daughter be a princess when she wed. She even wore a richly ornamented silver crown! "The Bridal Voyage in Hardanger", painted by Adolph Tidemand and Hans Fredrik Gude in 1848 and which now hangs in the National Gallery, shows this time-honored dress in all its detail. It has virtually become Norway's national painting.

On closer inspection you may be astounded at the treasure of silver displayed. The accessories are an integral part of the bunad – brooches, buttons and hooks, belts and buckles. Finely crafted knives, too, are used with the bunad. Notice also the complicated weaving techniques, decorations of minute beadwork, and time-consuming embroideries and specialized stitchwork. It takes hundreds of hours to make a bunad in the old-fashioned way!

Norsemen have been importing fine silver since before the Vikings, and they, in turn, valued it even more than gold. Their craftsmen, too, did fine work. The jewelry for the folk costumes which form the basis for the bunads, was inspired by that worn by wealthy city dwellers. In the decades prior to 1839, rural silversmiths were actually outlawed. The craft guilds in the towns and cities had a total monopoly of the market – at least in theory. Of course, local craftsmen did make copies, as well as create their own designs.

There is a rich symbolism in the jewelry. The stylized letters "AM", for instance, stand for Ave Maria, while the often repeated ring or circle symbolizes eternity and creation. Many of the larger brooches have a beautiful six-fold symmetry, like exquisite snowflakes.

Toward the end of the 19th century, the National Romantics inspired a new appreciation of the Norwegian peasant culture. Two women played a decisive role in revitalizing folk costume traditions: Hulda Garborg and Klara Semb. Since a proper bunad is based on the

Above: The traditional costumes are an essential element of Adolph Tidemand and Hans Fredrik Gude's painting, "Bridal Voyage in Hardanger", 1848. The National Gallery.

finery and everyday clothing worn by people in specific areas, each region in Norway now has its own bunad, sometimes with intriguing variations. The costumes worn by peasants were inspired by Renaissance clothing common on the continent in the 16th and 17th centuries; in some regions there is a continuous tradition extending right up to modern times, while the bunad of other areas may be a reconstruction based on rather sketchy historical material.

A comparison of bunads worn today with those in museums reveals the influence of modern fashions and materials. The blouses are thinner, the cut slightly adjusted, and the waist lowered.

No one is able to say exactly how many different bunads there are in Norway. Since this living folk tradition is not based on precise formulas, there are many variations on each of them.

Knitwear from Norway

Hand-knitted sweaters are extremely popular with foreigners visiting Norway, and the most attractive patterns are often knitted by a hundred thousand Norwegians. But what do we actually know of Norwegian knitting traditions and the history of knitting?

Detail from a pattern by Oleana, a producer of knitwear in Bergen which has explored alternative sources of inspiration.

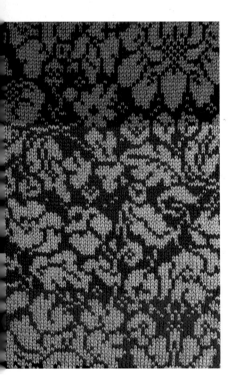

Religious illustrations from 14th century Southern Europe display the Virgin Mary knitting. But it is doubtful that the artists' intention was to portray the origins of knitting.

The earliest records of knitting come from Egypt and date from the end of the 10th century. Knitting techniques gradually spread through Europe and northward. In 16th century England, knitting schools were set up to help the poor find work, a model continued by Christian IV. Certain countries organized teams of knitters, often male, and the knitters were regarded as craftsmen.

The architectural dig at Bryggen, the wharf in Bergen, unearthed the remains of a knitted garment from the end of the 15th century. But it is difficult to say precisely when knitting arrived in Norway and Scandinavia. The first Norwegian records of people making a living from knitting come from 1630-40s Stavanger. As early as the 16th century, however, we find records of an extensive export of knitted socks and gloves from Iceland and the Faeroe Islands. In knitted working gloves, the wool was often strengthened with human hair.

The Norwegian farming culture promoted handmade products and cast shame on those who bought things they could make themselves. Knitting grew in popularity throughout all the social classes, even within the high society in towns and cities. In those days, there were no patterns or instructions, and great skill and experience were required to shape the garment to suit both the size and shape of the intended wearer, and current trend and tastes.

In Norway, there are many organized groups of women who knit and make other handicrafts to earn money for charities such as missionary societies. During the Russian invasion of Finland, a bitter cold winter, Norway started a huge campaign to knit warm garments for the Finnish soldiers. And during the Second World War, red woolen hats became such a well-known national symbol for Norway, that they were eventually prohibited by the German occupation forces.

Genuine Norwegian garments

Traditional Norwegian knitted garments all have strict geographical origins, but most local variations were first created in the 19th century.

It is often difficult to describe or define authentic Norwegian knitting patterns and designs. The popular eight-petaled rose, for example, can be seen on early imported nightgowns of knitted silk. This design is in fact international and can be found in folk art worldwide. Like a number of other geometric patterns, it seems archetypal. However, patterns which have been used over centuries, adapted, improved and integrated with other patterns, have become authentically Norwegian, irrespective of origins.

Some knitted garments are also adorned with intricate, colorful embroidery, often as borders. A number of these designs have been inspired by traditional Norwegian rose-painting. Buttons and hooks fashioned of pewter are also important, and they imitate the delicate silver jewelry worn with the national costume.

Today, sweaters and jackets and other knitted garments may be extremely colorful. A few generations ago, it was not common to use yarn spanning all the colors of the rainbow. Old garments in Bergen Museum, for instance, are knitted mostly of white and black wool. It was more common to use plant dyes for wool which was to be woven.

On old garments, most of the patterns occur on the bodice, upper back and arms. The lower part of a sweater, which was tucked into one's trousers on cold days, was usually left white – there was no need for time-consuming details there.

Earlier, the main purpose of knitwear was to keep warm while you were going about your tasks in the winter. Today, people more often knit or buy knitted garments because they are fashionable.

The way we knit, too, has changed. Norwegians use two knitting needles which are joined by a flexible rod. As a result, we are able to knit full circle and can avoid seams. It is actually possible to knit some sweaters without a single seam, but for the most part, the arms are knitted separately and then sewn on.

Today, designers are inspired by many sources – old brocade patterns, wrought-iron work and painted floral decorations.

Norwegian wool is strong and fortunately doesn't pill easily. Even synthetics such as microfiber are no longer considered a travesty in yarn blends. Exclusive yarn, especially for women's garments, may contain soft hairs of angora, cashmere or alpaca. For baby garments, yarn producers may blend in merino wool, a fine short-haired wool from warmer countries.

Olympic sweaters and new designs

Dale of Norway, one of western Norway's leading manufacturers of knitwear, created its first Olympic sweater in 1956. Since that date, Dale's Olympic sweaters have become a popular, colorful tradition which now also includes an annual World Championship sweater.

Nowadays, most knitters use patterns and instructions bought in yarn shops. The creation of new designs, once the craft of local villagers, is now carried out by professional designers.

Oleana, a company in Bergen, has gained popularity and awards for their exciting designs based on ancient Norwegian folk art and other untraditional sources. Their knitwear is noted for striking patterns and color combinations.

The quality of the wool

The continued popularity of knitted garments is mainly due to the numerous advantages of wool. Not only does it keep us warm, it also breathes well and absorbs moisture without staying wet. Moisture is led to the garment's surface, where it evaporates. And due to the lanolin content, dirt cannot stick to wool.

The dog may be man's best friend, but sheep are rather more important companions. Today, the spinning wheel and other tools used to make wool have become collectors' items.

Shopping for wool and woolen garments

For many years, hand-knitted sweaters have been among the most popular souvenirs for foreign tourists visiting Norway. But maybe you should think about buying Norwegian wool to take home with you. If you have a good eye for color combinations, you can create a unique garment. The shop assistants will be able to provide you with good advice.

Sweaters with Viking inspired patterns knitted of the softest wool are popular with children on festive occasions.

Houses of Worship
in Western Norway

At first glance, they resemble churches - white, simple, spartan - but they have no belltower, no resonating signals to call believers to worship. The bedehus as we Norwegians call our houses of worship, have a special social, theological and historical role.

Nowhere else in Norway are there so many houses of worship as in the four western counties. The first "bedehus" were built in the middle of the 19th century, but we have to go an additional century back in time if we are to shed light on their history.

In 1741 a royal ordinance was decreed to regulate religious assemblies outside churches. Essentially, it forbade laymen from holding religious meetings without the approval of the local priest.

Throughout the 19th century, the laymen's movement gathered strength and became a social and religious factor that could not be ignored. Even jailing Hans Nielsen Hauge, one of the most zealous laymen preachers, for ten years, was counterproductive. In 1842 the royal ban was lifted, after 101 years. Society had become more complex. And in this Age of Enlightenment, the court wanted to grant greater personal freedom in religious matters.

Adolph Tidemand's painting "Low Church Devotion", from 1852, captures the intensity of the belief which was the driving force of the laymen's movement. The movement was especially strong in the coastal regions.

A strong schism developed between the theologically conservative movement and the almost fossilized state church. Only after 1842 did one have permission to build houses of worship. Even so, in 1840 the first one was erected in Hjelmeland in Ryfylke. Many missionary organizations were established before the turn of the century.

Missionary organizations were the first to provide aid to families in Africa and Asia. It is striking that the most eager donors are those who have the least. Practical people provide practical aid – much of the money was used to build schools and hospitals, not just send out missionaries. Surprising to some, the Norwegian laymen's movement established schools, welfare work, and started magazines and newspapers and other media.

In Hordaland county, a new political party was established in 1933 – the Christian Democratic Party. The founders were firmly anchored in the layman's movent, although the party was soon being led by priests.

Like father and son

There are important differences between the interiors of churches and houses of worship. The latter have no altar rail, even though some do serve communion. In the early 20th century, many wanted to break with the Church. But their relationship is like that of a rebellious son who really seems unable to turn his back on his father. Today, the leaders of the laymen's movement are the most eager critics of the Church, but hey hesitate when it comes to leaving the good fold. For the same reason, meetings at the "bedehus" are rarely held in competition with church services. Many members of the congregation go to both! For others it is unthinkable to set their foot in a church.

At the back of the older houses of worship, there is an elevated gallery where curious observers may sit without being seen. Those who repented their sinful lives, could step down into the meeting hall and surrender their souls to God. There was far more room for tears and remorse here than in Lutheran churches. To the laymen's movement, dancing, alcohol and promiscuity were three of the most dangerous tempters and temptresses.

Those who accused the laymen preachers of being overly eager to pass judgment on others and of having a pitch-black view of life, rarely have first-hand experience from the houses of worship. Many key figures in Norwegian cultural life have received an upbringing centered in these houses of worship.

Today, most major villages have their own house of prayer, many of them constructed in recent decades. Some buildings belong to missionary organizations, others to the villages themselves. You might say they are a cultural counterpart to the youth centers. Pity the person who innocently suggests making room for both under the same roof!

For a Good Cause

They give of their time and devote their craft to a good cause. The knitting needles and crochet hooks are busy while they're chatting. If you don't know better, you might think they are survivors from a different age. But in fact, the women who contribute to the missionary organizations and other good causes have changed Norwegian society in decisive ways.

In 1844, Gustava Kjelland founded an entirely knew type of Christian association for women – local groups who produced textiles to generate income for the missionary organizations. Her idea spread like wildfire. Soon, thousands of such local groups were gathering women of all ages, from all walks of life, in villages and towns, on exposed islands and in mountain hamlets.

You might say that they used knitting needles and crochet hooks as weapons to defend themselves. You see, at that time, it was quite controversial for women to leave home and congregate without husbands or chaperones. But their cause was their alibi.

This movement did much more than raise funds for good causes and charities – which they still do. It gradually made a far-reaching impact. The closely knit groups led women into public work and other types of tasks as well. Soon, new associations with clear political intent were founded. These were instrumental in Norwegian women finally obtaining the right to vote in the 1913 national elections.

Meeting of the women's society on Remøy.

The Western Norwegian

The western Norwegian knows how to meet winter nights and spring storms. At times, the climate may seem inhospitable. Unending weeks of rain are enough to make anyone long for the sun and Mediterranean beaches. The very next moment, however, when the sun breaks through the cloud cover, the beauty of the landscape enchants us and makes us forget any notion of abandoning our chosen place.

A History of Rain Gear

In the west of Norway, you have three choices. You can stay indoors between 150 and 200 days each year. You can be a very wet masochist. Or you can protect yourself from the elements. As a result, western Norwegians were some of the first to develop effective rain gear.

In museums, there are 18th century leather garments that have been impregnated with oil, and there is every reason to believe this idea dates back much further. Since the dawn of time, people have used leather for warmth and protection. It is not unlikely that some of the first coastal hunters discovered that sealskin, for instance, had an exceptional ability to protect them when they had to wander through rain showers that might last for a week or two.

Capes have also been made of birch bark, a material traditionally used under turf roofs as well. A book illustration from 1832 shows the Swedish botanist, Karl von Linné, wearing such a cape.

The ceremonial cloak of bishops are supposedly derived from Roman rain gear. The Romans, a practical people in most matters, would protect themselves from the rain by wearing hooded, ankle-length robes. According to this theory, the shield – usually the sign of the cross – on the back of the bishops frocks are the vestiges of these hoods!

In England, Macintosh patented rubberized textiles in 1820. As a result, the company name has become synonymous with rain gear in Great Britain. Norway, however, was neither a colonial power nor was it even independent at this time – so large quantities of rubber were simply unaffordable.

In the town of Haugesund and on the coast of Møre in the northwest, companies started producing specialized clothing for fishermen in the mid-1800s – garments made of canvas impregnated with oil, preferably linseed oil. During World War II, when supplies of linseed oil were quite limited, producers had to find other alternatives. Asphalt oil and even cod liver oil resulted in odorous garments which, needless to say, did not have the best reputation.

Modern rain gear was introduced in the 1950s and the first PVC produced in 1951. Today, the factories in western Norway are closed down; the best known Norwegian producer of rain gear is Helly-Hansen, located in Moss in eastern Norway.

The Norwegian sardine canning industry owes at least part of its success on the export market to the pipe-smoking fisherman, in the yellow sou'wester, who has decorated their products since the early 1900s. Tiedemanns Tobaksfabrik, which still produces pipe and roll-your-own tobacco, was using the fisherman on their packaging decades before that again. These early advertisers were fully aware that this was a positive symbol which gave their products good associations. But no one seems to know who invented the fashionable and immensely practical headwear. At the end of the 19th century, Christian Krohg painted many scenes of fishermen – none of them, however, was a real western Norwegian.

Would we have harvested as much of the fruits of the sea without great rain gear? It's one of the most practical possessions of any western Norwegian, for work and play.

Tiny Rain Boots...

Small children in tiny rain boots and tiny sou'westers are a strange sight in the eyes of tourists who visit Fjord Norway. What in the world are the children doing outside in pouring rain? The children know the answer. While grownups may seek shelter, they wish to explore. Gleeful shrieks are the signs of joyful play. The child knows the freedom of water and, uninhibited, flows with the moment.

Moods of the Coast

The habitation of western Norway is concentrated along the coast. If we travel along the outermost coast, we can sense a long history. People settled here in order to be near the resources of the sea. Jetties have been built to protect houses as well as boats. In this barren landscape, there is often an utter lack of trees or bushes to shield anything from the wind. Some of the coastal settlements have been abandoned, others have built up new, successful trades or industries and are very viable, indeed.

Curious children aren't the only ones who explore the shoreline after a storm, to see what has been washed ashore. The play of light on the water, and the gentle clucking of waves under the quay or between the shore rocks are sensory impressions that have made lasting imprints on many of us.

We may see that seagulls have taken over an old warehouse or wharf building, as though it were their own. A generation or two ago, there was hectic activity here from before dawn until late at night during the fishing seasons. Some islands have population of wild goats, whose ancestors were livestock kept by farmers. The goat is a grateful animal to keep, managing outside year-round.

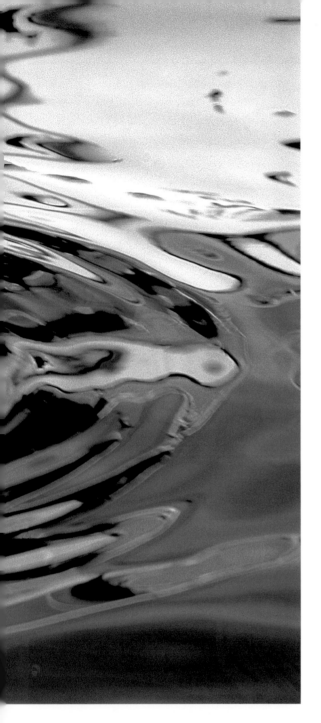

An old whaler may have a hard time understanding that his former trade is no longer politically correct. It's been a long time since anyone fired a harpoon from the prow of "Brødrene".

A coastal voyage reveals similarities between places north and south, but also telling variations – in architecture and vessel types, for instance. The old boats were developed for a variety of purposes and had different challenges when facing the wind and waves.

We may also find cause to reflect on some of the developments along the outer coast. A fishing village that attracted two thousand fishermen during the rich herring fisheries of the 1930s, may have recently been purchased as a holiday home by someone of much more wealth.

Traditional Farming

Treasures of the Sea

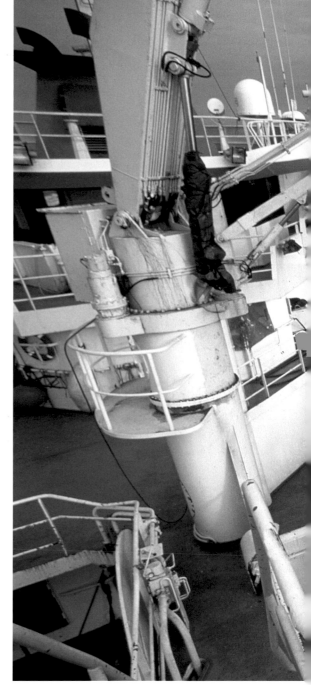

Many tourists who come to Norway are amazed at our fertile waters. It might seem you could even throw a bare, unbaited hook into the water and still haul up a good catch! The pictoglyphs show that even the earliest western Norwegians went fishing.

The fisheries of Fjord Norway have been radically changed by the invention of new types of fishing gear and new kinds of vessels. Boats equipped with engines, robust ocean trawlers, and other boats equipped with engines and echo sounders, enable fishermen to fish in waters frequented by fish far from the protected coast.

Times may have changed, but the work of a fisherman is still demanding. Since the late 1970s, the aquaculture industry has supplemented traditional fisheries.

Christmas Eve 1966 gave Norwegians good reason to celebrate. The first drops of oil were extracted from the Ekofisk sector, inaugurating an age of prosperity for the country.

Actually, we can thank the forests and wetlands for our riches. Our oil and gas deposits were formed mostly of the forests that grew three to four hundred million years ago.

New technologies have been developed to extrude oil from great depths below the continental shelf. Horizontal drilling is so precise that operators can reach small pockets of oil that might lie several kilometers from the oil platforms. But technology can't always replace old-fashioned cleverness. Mountain climbing techniques are now in widespread use when maintenance or surface treatment have to be carried out in difficult-to-reach places.

Take the Challenge!

Divers en route to their destination. It's far calmer below the churning waves.

You have to learn to read the shadows. They reveal tiny cracks, small overhangs – the holds for your hands and feet. Time has left its mark, scarring the smooth stone and leaving behind these minute edges on which you lever yourself up higher. The steep mountainsides have been here for aeons. Sharp rock presses into your hands, a keen reminder of your chosen challenge. On these age-old mountains, you can make your dreams come true.

The Norwegian climbing milieu abides by clear aesthetic and ethical principles. Leave no traces – no pegs, pitons or rope stubs. Change yourself, not the mountain. The mountains will be here long after the letters have faded on our gravestones.

William Cecil Slingsby was one of the main pioneers of climbing in Norway. As early as the 1880s, Slingsby and a group of other English climbers, explored a number of the areas which are most popular today.

Good climbing areas

You will find excellent climbing in most parts of Norway. One of the best known is the magnificent 1100 meter high Trollveggen rock face in Romsdalen. On its north face, you will find ice in the cracks even during the summer. In 1967, French climbers used 20 days to ascend via an excruciating direct route to the top! Not far from Trollveggen are the beautiful Sunnmøre Alps and the challenging Romsdal mountain range.

Close by the well-known Preikestolen (Pulpit Rock) southeast of Stavanger, you can find difficult climbs in Lysebotn and Kjerag.

A few meters above the ground

The risk may be negligible – you're less than five meters above the ground – but many consider bouldering to be the most demanding form of climbing. The sport is exercised on small cliffs or large boulders, which are both plentiful in the west of Norway.

You don't need much in the way of equipment – climbing shoes, a talcum bag and your own body. Ropes and fasteners are banned. Bouldering makes extreme demands on your physical abilities and technical maste-

Rafting on the Valldøla river really does demand full concentration.

ry of the art of climbing. Not to mention your concentration. While a climbing route on a mountainside may have two or three cruxes, the decisive points used to rate its difficulty, every moment is decisive for a boulderer. And it's a form of climbing that caters to an audience – the unbelievers among us can study how in the world these acrobats defy gravity!

Ice climbing

Some people find a perverse joy in rappelling down waterfalls – it's a cold and wet sport. During the winter, many waterfalls freeze into impressive columns of ice, some of them hundreds of meters high. Only a few have ever been climbed.

Another challenge for experienced adventurers is to climb the ice falls of glaciers. This is definitely not for novices!

From a bird's eye view

If you perch on a craggy peak and gaze down at the luminous sea of clouds flowing around the mountain tops nearby, you may feel as if you have grown wings! For some, the feeling is not enough – they stretch their wings to go paragliding or hang-gliding from mountain peaks. With the right wind and good technique, you can enjoy a bird's eye view for hours; some have flown from Voss all the way to the island of Osterøy.

When the people of Bergen look up, they can often see paragliders soaring from Mount Ulriken, the highest of the seven peaks surrounding Bergen.

Most of your friends may have a snowboard by now, but perhaps you can be the first to try "skysurfing"? It's simple, really – you throw yourself out of a plane at high altitude with a snowboard secured to your boots. Then you just ride the wind until you have to release your parachute. Come to think of it, straightforward parachuting, too, gives an unforgettable impression of the landscape that rushes up to meet you. There are active clubs at Voss, in Bergen and in Molde.

To jump into the abyss

A few years ago, Norwegian base jumpers had to keep their passion a secret, or risk losing their parachuter's license. Today their sport is tolerated, if not exactly approved, by the Norwegian Sports Federation. The time margins are tight at best, but the introduction of better equipment and better training has made it a safer pastime in recent years.

From the Kjerag mountains in the Lysefjord, base jumpers can enjoy an impressive 20 second free fall.

Experienced skiers and snowboarders search far from the beaten track to make sure they find virginal snow.

Exploring the
Briksdalsbreen glacier.

the river" – it's no use fighting the force of the water. Team spirit is of the essence as you race down the waters in a raft, coordinating every movement. Among the best rivers are Raundalselva and Strandaelva, Jølstra and Breimselva. There are a number of companies offering organized rafting trips where safety is top priority.

Rafting may be fun for a while, but experienced connoisseurs of water sports usually choose the kayak as their vessel. It responds far quicker, allows better control and brings you into closer rapport with the rushing river.

Some kayakers have the privilege of seeing wilderness inaccessible to anyone else. Tourists may be familiar with the Nærøyfjord, but the Nærøydal river is an even more stunning experience. The white, round stones on the river bottom glow through the green, crystal-clear water. Another favorite river is Brandset-elva, where an impressive series of obstacles make it ideal for extreme sport. We wouldn't be surprised if this becomes a venue for a future world championship in river kayaking.

The last four or five kilometers of Raundalselva, before it flows into Vangsvatnet lake, are perfect for beginners. Where the Vosso river leaves this lake, there are unusual currents that attract freestyle kayakers. If the water flow is just right, a large standing wave is formed, which you can challenge again and again, thanks to a back-setting current.

A focus on extreme sport

It's really no surprise that an increasing number of companies are realizing the value of extreme sports as an ingredient in their team-building programs. Extreme challenges inspire bonding and cooperation that enable companies to better meet the daunting challenges in their world of business as well.

The week of Midsummer's Eve, Voss is the place to be. That is when an annual event attracts practitioners of extreme sports from around the world.

Karlsgråtind in Romsdal, much further north, is considered the safest site in Northern Europe, thanks to the large overhang and excellent landing conditions. Jumping from the scenic Trollveggen, however, is strictly forbidden, after a series of serious accidents and expensive rescue operations. To base jumpers throughout the world, Trollveggen enjoys a status on par with El Capitan in Yosemite National Park in California – but there, too, jumping is banned.

Some base jumpers look like flying squirrels as they soar. A special wing suit, in which base jumpers stretch a membrane between their arms and legs, filling cells with air to actually form a wing profile, allows them to double their time in free fall.

Wet and satisfied

Forget artificial water slides. The proper place for water sports is in the wilderness. Equipped with a helmet, wet suit, life vest and plenty of courage, an increasing number of people choose to follow experienced guides down river canyons. Sliding down smooth stone chutes, rushing down roaring rapids and jumping from cliffs into deep culps provides an adrenaline kick for many enthusiasts.

Rafting is one of the wildest ways to visit the foaming Norwegian rivers. You have to learn to "read

Even bicyclists can get to the summit of Kjerag ridge.

A History of
Salmon Fishing

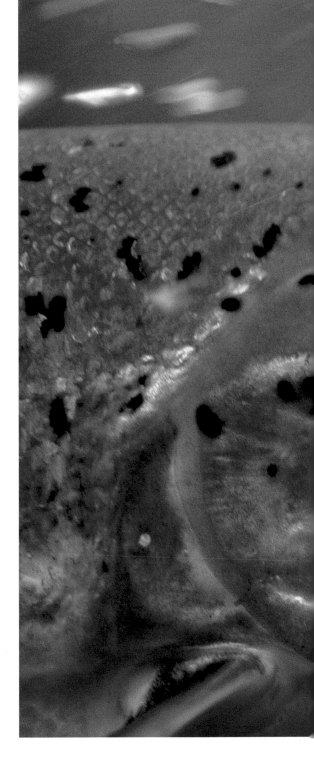

It's been thousands of years since someone prepared the first salmon dinner over the fire in the west of Norway. Petroglyphs at Honhammerneset in Nordmøre attest to the importance of salmon already in the Stone Age.

Each summer, salmon return from the sea to spawn in our rivers. The miracle of it all is that each fish somehow manages to find its way back to the precise spot where it hatched. Some researchers believe salmon are using a most refined sense of smell, and that young salmon who swim out to sea a little earlier, leave a fragrant track which mature salmon can follow upstream.

Salmon are powerful fish – they have to be to fight their way up these fierce rivers. They even manage to traverse strong rapids and small waterfalls. Along their route, however, there are watchful fishermen waiting for their opportunity.

Patient moments

English lords have been fishing the rivers of western Norway for more than a century. They were astonished to catch specimens of almost 35 kilos. Hooking such a monster is asking for a battle which may last many hours. Naturally, the first aristocratic arrivals didn't wait long before negotiating long-term leases!

Some places, surprising methods have been used to catch salmon. Industrious souls might place a large net at the entrance to a narrow fjord arm. Then the fishermen would sit in huts elevated on poles. As soon as the salmon swam into the net bag, they would pull a rope to seal it off. A salmon trap requires far less attention. Other places, people have actually stood right by the falls and hit the salmon with clubs as they tried jumping through the air.

Apparently, Viking merchants were the first to export Norwegian salmon. The fish is well-suited for drying, smoking or salting. Various historical sources document the importance of salmon. Some farmers even paid their taxes with salmon.

The incomparable Mr. Jones

Stone Age fishermen may have acquired a taste for salmon, but fishing for sport is a relatively modern phenomenon. The beauty of the surrounding landscape has been a key ingredient treasured by every angler who has come to Fjord Norway. Since English aristocrats came here in the 19th century, more than one travel journalist, Lord, or retired officer has had the joy of standing by a pristine river, knowing that they were probably the very first anglers to cast a fly from their chosen spot.

One of the first guide books on freshwater angling in Fjord Norway, was published by a certain Londoner named Mr. Jones, who both manufactured and sold fishing gear. Mr. Jones understood successful marketing, and made decisive contributions toward making our rivers even more popular with wealthy travelers. A side effect of all this, of course, was that Mr. Jones sold more fishing gear than ever.

Don't misunderstand – the English hardly have a monopoly in regards to their interest in salmon fishing. The Norwegian royal family consists of eager fishermen, as do many families with blue blood from other countries. Although you don't have to document your pedigree to challenge the salmon, you do have to have your finances in order. Salmon fishing is not exactly an inexpensive sport.

No true angler would ever dare try to calculate the real price of salmon fishing, in terms of price per kilo. An increasing number of salmon fishermen are now using hooks without a barb; as a result, they can release the fish without injuring it. Those who do keep their catch have quite a feast to look forward to, a feast best shared with others.

A sublime meal

The secret to a wonderful salmon meal is to make sure the salmon you're cooking stays juicy. Salmon must never be overcooked or fried long over strong heat. Leading chefs will tell you that grilled salmon is actually tastiest when it is almost raw inside.

Salmon is healthy, too! Medical research has shown the benefits of Omega 3 fatty acid, which among other things helps reduce the risk of heart disease. But don't let the doctor convince you to take Omega 3 tablets – why miss out on a pink gourmet meal?

Grilled, steamed or poached salmon provides a mouth-watering meal. Smoked salmon is ideal for tasty sandwiches. Some say it's even better on lefse. Others insist that marinated salmon served with a mild mustard sauce is the epitome of a salmon meal!

And the salmon fisherman? He or she is likely to say that the finest way to enjoy salmon is straight from the hook to the fire. While they're practicing telling their fish stories, of course. Things haven't changed all that much these last three or four thousand years.

The Fish, the Fly and the Silence

Even fishermen who return empty-handed often have a smile of satisfaction on their faces. Fishing can be pure meditation – the silence, concentration and surrounding nature. Especially fly fishing is a fine way to rid oneself of inner noise and knots.

How to judge a fly? It's a good fly when it catches fish!" says Bjørn Helgesen rather matter-of-factly. He feels privileged – his hobby is his livelihood. A large assortment of flies, large and small, and spanning all the colors of the rainbow, lie on the table in the specialty shop in Bergen. A good flymaker is always open to new ways of approaching his craft.

The fly-dresser

There are essentially two types of flies. Imitators tempt the fish by resembling insects they eat, while the only purpose of attractors is to trigger deep instincts that may be very difficult to understand. "Unfortunately, attractors are still more common, but this is changing," says Bjørn Helgesen. He is a purist. "You may catch fewer fish with imitator flies, but they're bigger. Besides, it's a more natural way to fish." The insect net is an important tool, enabling the flyfisher to study which insects frequent the river where he or she is fishing.

Salmon actually stop feeding as they swim upstream to their spawning grounds. That's why you have to use attractors for salmon fishing in the rivers. Irritation or other triggered reactions make salmon snap at the fly. Trout fishing is different.

One of the most renowned fly-dresser is Frank Myhre Hansen. He makes his flies the old way – traditional methods and no substitute materials. A fly-dresser may make great efforts to obtain feathers of a certain exotic bird, a tuft of rabbit hair or a bit of squirrel tail.

An expert rod maker, such as Vidar Tøsse in Bergen, also has quite a challenge. He has to seek the right balance between flexibility and stiffness, and the proper length of rod. This is customized not just to the species of fish the angler is trying to hook, but to the fisherman's temper and personal preferences. Tøsse uses both traditional split cane and high-technology materials such as carbon fiber.

Surprising to all but connoisseurs, an increasing number of fishermen are using hooks without a barb. "That enables you to release the fish without harming it," explains Helgesen. "I think you have to be a fisherman to understand that."

Fly fishing is a long and noble tradition. Macedonian sources mention fly fishing as early as 130 AD. Amazingly the most quoted book in the English House of Commons is neither the Bible nor the laws of the empire, but a book on angling written by Isaac Walton in the 17th century!

The best fishing spots

Some of the best trout rivers in western Norway are the Aurlandselva, Eidselva Stryn, Etne, Suldalslågen, Årdalselva and Osenelva. Aurlandselva is probably the very best of them. Many anglers feel a sense of humility when fishing there. It's a classic river where you have a good chance of catching the fish of your life – quite a few have. Like other rivers in western Norway, the water is crystal clear. That makes it a real challenge, because the fish are easily spooked.

Wealthy foreigners and English lords still rent some of the best sections of our rivers. It is said, however, that all distinctions of class cease above the tree line or when you're fishing.

There are many lesser know tributaries and small rivers where anglers may fish in peace. "I hate fishing in a crowd. Finding good spots off the beaten path is a bit like searching for exquisite, affordable wine. Nevertheless I share information on my fishing spots with other fishermen. There are only a few places I keep to myself, where I know I can be alone and enjoy true silence."

Avoiding conversation

It may take as little as five or six hours of concentrated training before someone is able to cast halfway decently. But that's just the beginning. A good fly fisherman has to be able to "read" the river. The fish may be standing by large rocks or other spots where it feels protected, but can still move quickly to catch edible tidbits that float by. They also prefer to be near the banks, where they don't have to fight the current so much.

Fishermen require good imaginations. They have to predict the reaction of the fish, know its biology, needs and behavior. A good fly fisherman has been "studying"

for years. One of the main challenges is simply getting to the fishing spot silently and unnoticed. The fish you're after hasn't grown huge by ignoring danger signals and taking chances needlessly.

Fly fishermen don't make much noise amongst travelers. They come and go almost unnoticed, perhaps with a telltale transport tube for their rod. Some come from other Scandinavian countries, others from England or Germany, or even from the USA.

"I really don't feel conversation and fishing mix. Fishing requires silence and concentration. Silence and the beauty of nature, those are the most important ingredients for me. Then, of course, the cup of coffee and a cigarette while I'm waiting for the right moment, tranquilly waiting for the light of dawn. As you gain experience, catching fish really does become the least important aspect of it all."

Fish doesn't come much fresher than straight from the lake into the frying pan. Lake Nåsavatnet, Nordmøre.

The rhythm of jazz fills the air at the market place in Molde.

Festivals

The Vikings were good at finding an excuse to hold a lively feast or festival. When music was played and stories were told for days and nights on end, people would come from afar to join the fun. In that respect, times haven't changed much.

Summer is the hottest festival season. For those who appreciate folk music, a highlight is the Førde Folk Music Festival. Stavanger is well-known for its International Chamber Music Festival, where concerts are even held in the 13th century monastery at Utstein, on an island north of the city.

There are also a number of historical plays, most of them performed at outdoor sites where the dramas really took place centuries ago – such as at Moster, Kinn, Herøy and the barony in Rosendal. Even if you don't understand a word, it's worth going just to enjoy the setting!

The Bergen Festival dates back to a music festival that Edvard Grieg helped to organize in 1898, in conjunction with a trade fair. Even he met loud resistance and stepped on obviously sensitive toes when he wanted to invite an orchestra from Amsterdam. Parallel events include concerts of contemporary music and a jazz festival. Later in the summer, the Eggstokk Festival provides a setting for many young, ambitious musicians.

The opera in Kristiansund, the oldest in Norway, is the central venue when this northwestern town arranges its annual Opera Festival – which, by the way, consists of far more than opera.

The jazz festivals in Voss and Haugesund have a charm all their own. But when it comes to jazz, the town where it really swings is Molde, in the middle of July.

Anglers and fishermen deserve their own celebrations. The fishing festivals in Florø and Stavanger are only two of those that are better known. The rich and colorful coastal culture of western Norway becomes very visible during the Harbor Days in Haugesund, the Market Days in Bergen, and the Skude Festival in Skudeneshavn.

Ballett dancers, Bergen.

Hundreds of enthusiasts from the districts near Bergen, all wearing proper attire, add authenticity the annual Market Days.

A good festival should be tasted! The Norwegian Food Festival in Ålesund is held in conjunction with the national chef competition. The Gastronomic Institute in Stavanger makes a hearty contribution to the Norwegian Fruit and Salmon Festival in Hjelmelandsvågen, a memorable and tasty experience. In Vik in Sogn og Fjordane county there is, believe it or not, even a festival dedicated to the pungent cheese called gammalost.

Certainly this is all proof enough that the descendants of Vikings, too, are good at finding an excuse for partying. When the many-faceted culture of western Norway is shared, people gather with long-lasting smiles. Even in small villages and towns, you are likely to find very worthwhile festivals. Just be sure to cross off the right date on your calendar.

From the historical play on the island of Herøy.

Museums
- Treasures
of History

What is a museum, really? Even though the answer might seem obvious, this was one of the central questions at the international museum conference held in Stavanger in 1995.

Stavanger is known for its Cannery Museum.

O ur museums are the treasures of history, and to many of us, one of the most valued parts of our common heritage. A good museum has a multiple focus: preservation, research and communication with its public. The resources and imagination allotted to these areas may vary. In recent decades, communication, and our view of what qualifies as a treasure, has changed radically.

The very first museum in western Norway was Bergen Museum, established in 1821. It was a museum of natural history and a research institution which later grew into the University of Bergen.

Rogaland

Many archaeologists dream of bringing the past back to life again. That is exactly what the Stavanger Museum of Archaeology has managed to do. The prehistoric village

at Forsand and the Iron Age farm at Ullandhaug are more than reconstructions. At both places, you can experience people in period dress engaged in various crafts or going about their tasks. At Nærbø south of Stavanger, there is a museum which offers insight into the rich agricultural history of the region. And at Avaldsnes on the island of Karmøy, a Viking farm has been recreated down to the tiniest detail. The Stavanger Museum of Archaeology has an extensive and fascinating collection.

The Fayance Museum in Egersund displays the special stoneware produced in this southern town for 122 years and as recently as 1979. Stavanger owes its wealth to herring and oil. The Norwegian Canning Museum casts light on a special chapter of our history. The Norwegian Oil Museum is a recent newcomer well worth a long visit.

Those who visit the Rogaland County Museum of Art should take time to enjoy the beautiful surround-

ings as well. The jewel in the museum is the large collection of paintings and drawings by Lars Hertervig, one of the most peculiar Norwegian artists of the 19th century.

Hordaland

The Hardanger Folk Museum has taken into use new means of communication. This museum's greatest resource may well be its amazing network of local experts and supporters, evidenced by its many branches. One of them is SS Mathilde, a Hardanger schooner built in 1884, and which sails with changing exhibitions.

The Heathlands Center at Lygra focuses on a cultural landscape formed through four thousand years. Today, this particular landscape is almost gone.

Bryggen Museum in Bergen chose a highly original way to preserve what archaeologists unearthed after a fire destroyed a major part of the old wharf. They

Above: The Oil Museum in Stavanger was designed by Lunde & Løseth, who competed with other architects. It opened in May, 1999.

Checkmate, a manned "underwater helicopter" was used on oil installations in the 1970s.

Whale skeleton,
Bergen Museum.

erected an award-winning building around the excavations. UNESCO has recognized the colorful history of nearby Bryggen, and its role as virtually a living museum. For added insight, the Hanseatic Museum is a must. Past Bryggen is a well-preserved fortress and the only royal hall dating back to the early Middle Ages.

There is also a rewarding concentration of art museums around Bergen's central lake, now with a common name – the Bergen Museum of Art. The institution has expanded into the distinctive old headquarters of the local power company.

If you have a special interest, you will probably find The Buekorps Museum, the Leprosy Museum and the Museum of Technology. The composers Edvard Grieg and Harald Sæverud have both been honored with their own museums. Troldhaugen is one of the most popular in Fjord Norway.

The Directorate of Cultural Heritage put its best craftsmen on the job and saved no expense when Damsgård Manor was restored in the mid 1990s. The result is exemplary, even the well-kept Renaissance garden.

The barony in Rosendal is widely known for its park-like grounds and its large rose garden. The barony, which housed the local aristocracy, is now a cultural center and treasured by people throughout the region. Every summer, concerts are held here, as well as historical plays.

The Norwegian Industrial and Hydroelectric Museum deserves its very own chapter. It tells the story of early industrialization in a spell-binding way.

Wounds may heal, but World War II made its mark on many towns and villages in western Norway. The residents of Telavåg were collectively punished when two German soldiers were found dead, and it was discovered that the village was a base for clandestine boat traffic to and from the Shetlands. The men were sent abroad to a concentration camp, while the women were incarcerated in Norway.

Sogn og Fjordane

The Heiberg Collection, better known as Sogn Folk Museum, focuses on the fjord and the coastal culture. It's easy to use a day just to explore the old vessels. Even though the boats of the Coastal Museum in Florø are in dry-dock, a pier has been built to create an integrated illusion. The museum also has a large exhibit on oil technology and oil extraction, using the Snorre platform as an illuminating example.

There is a large collection of old buildings at the outdoor Nordfjord Museum. One of the best preserved vessels of its type, the schooner SS Holvik, is the pride of the museum.

Those who appreciate the paintings of Nikolai Astrup, would do well to visit the farm where he spent his life and made most of his paintings. The skilled sculptor, Anders Svor, may have lived in the shadow of Gustav Vigeland, but he was just as skilled and certainly deserves his own museum. The contemporary artist, Ludwig Eikaas, has also been honored with his own museum, displaying many of his idiosyncratic, drawings, paintings and sculptures.

Children frolicking freely at Sunnfjord Museum in Førde.

There is a fine fisheries
museum on the island of
Hjertøya outside Molde.

Møre og Romsdal

Klipfish and boatbuilding occupy two important
sections of Nordmøre Museum in Kristiansund. This
museum, too, has several branches. Boatbuilders are
still practicing their ancient craft at the historical
Mellemværftet shipyards.

The Art Nouveau Center in Ålesund celebrated the
dawn of the third millennium by moving into the old
stone building which once housed the pharmacy. The
original population center lies 4 km east of Ålesund,
where Sunnmøre Museum is located now. This outdoor
museum has about 50 old buildings and copies of many
ancient ships.

You need a car to experience the many branches of
the Romsdal Museum – the vicarage at Nesse, Fisheries
Museum at Hjertøy, Textile Manufacture Museum in
Isfjorden, Rødven village museum and the museum at
Bø.

The Ivar Aasen Center in Volda celebrates one of the
worlds greatest linguists. It is largely thanks to him that
the rural dialects survive in written form as well as in
many spoken variations.

In awe before the largest
tank at Atlanterhavsparken
- the aquarium in Ålesund.

Edvard Grieg
- after the Sound Fades

Edvard Grieg may have measured only 1.52 meters, but his greatness as a composer and an intellectual must not be underestimated. His great feat was to unite Norwegian folk music with the new Romantic music of the continent, thus placing Norway firmly on the musical world map for all time. Grieg's music is imbued with an unusually rich melodic expression and vitality.

Music lovers the world over listen to Grieg and picture in their mind's eye fjords and mountains, dark forests and crystal clear rivers, trolls, beguiling milkmaids and lively dancing to the fiddle.

On the recommendation of Ole Bull, the famous violinist from Bergen, Grieg was sent to the Leipzig Conservatory in 1858, when he was just 15. Due to a severe lung infection which permanently damaged his left lung, his studies suffered a lengthy break. Despite his illness, he was a keen walker all his life, and would often set out on long trips in the mountains around Bergen, and in the Hardanger area where he loved to listen to the many folk songs. In 1869, he wrote "25 folk songs and dances", Opus 17, dedicated to Ole Bull.

Grieg remained faithful to the dissonance of the double-stringed Hardanger fiddle when he composed folk music for the pianoforte, and he managed to keep the rhythmic force of the fiddle intact. This is particularly evident in Opus 72, based on the airs of fiddler Knut Dale, who had asked Grieg to write down his tunes for posterity.

In the summer of 1868, just 25 years old, he composed what is now commonly considered his masterpiece – the Piano Concerto in A Minor – one of the most frequently played piano concertos. It quickly gained him worldwide renown.

At the age of 24, Edvard married his cousin, Nina Hagerup. Nina's mother, who was opposed to the marriage, protested that: "He is nothing and has nothing, and he writes music which no one wants to hear." Like many other mothers-in-law, she is now forgotten.

Symphonies in birdsong

Grieg's home on Troldhaugen in Bergen was built in 1885. Today it is open to the public, and during the summer concerts are held in the villa or in the nearby concert hall. It is a truly unique experience to hear Grieg's music performed on his old Steinway grand piano, in his own living room.

Like many composers, Grieg required absolute peace and quiet when composing. He built his composer's cottage below the villa, with a beautiful view of the fjord. There the only sound to disturb his work was, in his own words, "the bird song, which embodies sufficient themes for 27 symphonies and 24 operas".

Despite this, Grieg composed only one symphony and one unfinished opera. He mastered shorter pieces, in particular songs and lyrical works for the piano. He composed his songs for his wife Nina, who he believed to be their only true interpreter.

The majority of his songs have lyrics from Norwegian and Danish poets, including H. C. Andersen. This became problematic when the composer wanted his music to reach German or English audiences. He once dryly remarked: "It appears that few publishers value a good translation as highly as a cheap one."

Henrik Ibsen asked him to write music to his dramatic poem, Peer Gynt. The resulting 26 compositions made the premiere of this work in 1876 a unique success.

Grieg the letter writer

Grieg was a keen letter writer. In the course of his life he wrote no less than 20 000 letters to family and friends, an average of 12 letters a week. Some believe many letters are co-addressed to posterity.

Edvard Grieg was one of the few composers who enjoyed fame and renown while still alive. He was also much in demand as a guest conductor at many of Europe's prominent symphony orchestras. On such events, he always took his loyal friend with him, right onto the podium – an increasingly worn good-luck frog which he kept in his pocket.

A human being first and foremost

Grieg also became noted for his social conscience. To the dismay of French authorities, he canceled a concert in Paris in protest against the Dreyfuss issue, in which a French Jew had been falsely accused of espionage. When Grieg finally returned to Paris years later, and climbed onto the podium to conduct, many members of the audience whistled and jeered. But Grieg simply turned his back to them, lifted his baton, and stifled the voice of complaint with his intense, clamorous tones.

Grieg would not accept his compositions being treated as background music. When playing for King Edward VII, he interrupted the music twice because the English monarch was conversing loudly with his companions.

Grieg maintained that "You must first be a human being. All true art is born from human nature."

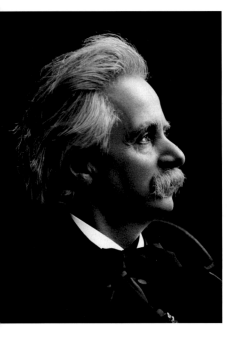

The Atonal Composer -
Fartein Valen

The changing moods of the western Norwegian landscape were of immense importance to the composer Fartein Valen (1887-1952), both musically and spiritually. Like the dominant national romantic composers of the day, to which his works were an immense contrast, Valen drew inspiration from the surrounding landscape – not least of all near the farm in Valevåg where he spent the final and most productive part of his life.

As his music matured, his melodies grew more chromatic and atonal; they no longer had the major and minor keys as references. It is for this revolutionary break that Fartein Valen is accorded an important place in the history of Western music.

Fartein Valen must have had unshakable faith in his creative work. He never cowered in the face of the many harsh attacks on him and his music, nor did he try to rebut the many critics amongst the members of the music establishment. But he did not meet only adversity; in 1935, the Norwegian Parliament awarded him the Artist's Stipend that allowed him to fully focus on his composition. In 1938 he moved from Oslo – which, like Grieg, he never truly appreciated – back to the family farm in Valevåg. Here he lived and worked, in quietude, until his death in 1952. These fourteen years were his most productive.

The house was furnished in a simple way; there was not even a gramophone. The garden received far more attention. Here he cultivated and bred hundreds of different roses. He gave each of them a name, often in honor of composers and artists of the past. Valen's rose garden was the inspiration for Pastorale, Opus 11.

Ode to Solitude, Opus 35, was inspired by the nearby screes where he often walked. Opus 20, The Cemetery By the Sea, is written in memory of the cholera victims buried in a graveyard near Valestrand. All of these works are so-called symphonic poems, orchestral works in one movement, a compositional form preferred by Valen.

Valen subscribed to several foreign newspapers to keep abreast on world events. When war broke out in Europe, he realized Norway was vulnerable. But when he one day saw a snow-white bird on a stone near the house – perhaps an albino – he took it as a sign that Norway would persevere in the trying times to come.

This sign inspired his magnificent Intermezzo for Piano, Opus 36.

Fartein Valen's library could hardly be described as provincial. He mastered nine languages and set to music poems by Goethe, Paul Valéry, Walt Whitman, Keats and Spencer – to mention a few.

Many of Valen's polyphonic compositions echo the music of Johann Sebastian Bach. Not so strange, really; Fartein Valen inaugurated each day by playing chorales of the great composer on his piano. Like his models, Bach and Bruckner, Valen wrote his music for the glory of God.

The legendary Canadian pianist Glenn Gould presented his recording of Fartein Valen's Second Piano Sonata, Opus 38, with the words: "I have found a great world composer."

Fartein Valen's groundbreaking music is much appreciated by other composers and musicians throughout the world.

The Landscape Painters

A painting often provides a truer impression of the landscape than a photograph. Perhaps this is because the painter, to a greater degree, is able to select, interpret and distill, to peel away secondary details and to concentrate on the essential.

It is somewhat ironic that it was Johan Christian Dahl, born in Bergen in 1788, who came to revolutionize Norwegian art. He left Norway, 23 years old, to study art in Copenhagen, and later Dresden where he became a professor. Dahl visited Norway only five times and was 38 on his first journey home. Before that, he painted his "Norwegian" landscapes from memory.

Western Norway seen from Dresden

Despite his geographic distance, he hardly has his equal when it comes to capturing the landscape of western Norway. If we study his paintings in the National Gallery in Oslo, or in other museums, we might be led to believe that Dahl apprenticed to one of the great Dutch or English masters. Actually, that's not far from the mark; the young artist spent long hours in museums trying to wrest the secrets from the Old Masters.

Dahl's greatest teacher, however, was nature itself. Neither botanists, geologists or meteorologists are able to find faults in his depictions of the landscape and vegetation, the sea and the sky. In fact, his precision enables botanists to identify the plant species shown in his paintings!

Dahl made hundreds of sketches and studies of the landscape when he was traveling. He must have felt quite a sense of urgency when he visited Norway – the trembling line of some drawings indicate that he must have made them while riding a horse or a wagon!

The landscapes of J.C. Dahl contain all the elements visitors associate with western Norway – foaming rivers, roaring waterfalls, dazzling glaciers, towering mountains, and what we now call the cultural landscape. It is no exaggeration to claim that it was Dahl who opened the eyes of Norwegians to the beauty of the wilderness of the West.

A different forest

The branches of the trees painted by Lars Hertervig (1830–1902) often seem more like roots, as though they were drawing essential nourishment from the air and the light itself. Hertervig's trees express a powerful vitality. Some of them have the dignity that comes from defying centuries of storms. Unlike no other Norwegian artist, Hertervig invites us to wander in a primal forest.

Lars Hertervig: "Motif from Borgøy". 1867. 61,5 x 69,5 cm. The National Gallery.

Lars Hertervig grew up in a poor family on the island of Borgøya in northern Rogaland, and he probably drew and painted this landscape more than any other. When he was only five years old, he would use charcoal to draw on bits of driftwood that he found along the shore.

In some of Hertervig's paintings, there appear to be two sources of light, something that reinforces our feeling of peering into a dream or a different world, even though his work is very figurative. Perhaps that is just what the artist did. Hertervig struggled with such severe psychological problems that he had to interrupt his art studies in Düsseldorf and return home, to seek treatment in an asylum. When he was released, few people took him seriously as an artist.

There is no escaping the symbolism of some of the elements in his paintings. Animals and human figures seem to participate in a dream, perhaps moving through the air in idyllic forests. Sometimes his trees seem to dance, other times to twist in inner turmoil. There are also paintings that consist solely of clouds and sky. Toward the end of his life, Hertervig painted – like Vincent van Gogh, who was also labeled "insane" – paths that suddenly end.

As a poor artist, Lars Hertervig would paint on any suitable surface he could find. In one of his paintings, the logo of a tobacco company in Oslo shines like a radiant underwater sun, albeit with a lion in its center!

Many people who visit the Rogaland County Museum of Art in Stavanger are astonished to realize that some of his paintings, which they may have seen reproduced in books, measure only 10 x 13 cm.

Hertervig also made his own paper from cardboard scraps, old newspapers and wallpaper. This poses quite a nightmare for museum curators, who of course wish to preserve his work for future generations.

Only on rare occasions could Hertervig afford paint in oil on canvas. For the most part, he used watercolors or gouache, or settled for making drawings.

He may have been destitute at times, but his pride was intact. When the mayor of Stavanger, the well-known author Alexander Kielland, sent a representative of the city to offer Hertervig larger and more comfortable quarters, the artist politely declined. Even in his worst distress, he refused gifts, though he willingly traded his artwork for food or other things he needed or sold them for a modest sum. Hertervig also gave away many paintings to friends or people he liked.

The painter from Jølster

While J.C. Dahl seemed content with trying to portray the landscape as accurately as possible, we sense that Nikolai Astrup (1880–1928) is an animist who wants to make the very landscape itself come alive. Astrup's colors, his energy and brush strokes make the mountains and fjords just as animated as the trees and flowers.

Astrup carries forth a testimony to the living landscape, to a spirit which seems all around us. It would seem that he considered painting an almost religious act.

No other Norwegian artist has been so strongly bound to one place. With few exceptions, his subjects were painted on the family farm in Jølster, or in the area nearby.

His intense colors, and at times non-naturalistic sense of form, may give the impression that Astrup was a naive painter. Not so – Astrup studied art both in Christiania (now Oslo) and in Paris. And on closer inspection, his palette is not even exaggerated. Those who have truly seen the vibrant greens when the sun breaks out after a rain shower, or witnessed the flowering fruit trees of late spring, are more likely to nod their heads in recognition or simply stand there in silent awe of Astrup's mastery.

A return to the landscape

Many other landscape artists are worth a closer study – Kitty Kielland, for instance, who was the first artist to discover the marshlands of southwestern Norway. It was here she painted some of her very best paintings.

Tidemand and Gude have become such a central concept in the art history of the 19th century that we sometimes forget that they were two artists, not one.

Nikolai Astrup: "Midsummer Eve Bonfire". 1912. 89 x 105. National Gallery.

Johan Christian Dahl: "From Stalheim".
190 x 246 cm. National Gallery.

Adolph Tidemand was a fine observer of the customs and costumes of rural life, while Hans Gude concentrated on the dramatic landscape. Together, these two easterners captured elements and qualities of western Norway in paintings that have become paramount examples of the National Romantic movement. Their best known work is "Bridal Voyage on the Hardangerfjord". Artistically, however, they don't come close to the mastery of Dahl.

Bent Tunold, too, is in a class by himself when it comes to conveying the light and moods of the landscape. In many respects he was overshadowed by Nikolai Astrup. They painted similar subjects. Tunold was more impressionistic, but his color scale was dominated by grays, browns and greens. He preferred tranquil scenery to storms, and grayish fog to sunlit brilliance.

We are never in doubt as to the inspiration and visual source material of a contemporary artist such as Knut Rumohr, even though his landscapes are highly abstracted. His huge canvases seem both monumental and expressionistic, and the use of pure colors is one of his most important devices.

It is also fascinating to see western Norway through the eyes of foreign artists; one of the most interesting is Olivier Debré. This French artist, who died recently, grasped the essence of the region's special light. The simplification and lyrical abstraction in some of his works is astonishing. Debré visited western Norway and probably spent more time here than J.C. Dahl did in his adult life.

At the Edge of the Light
– at the Edge of Darkness

The painter Ørnulf Opdahl lives on the northeastern shore of Godøy island, west of Ålesund. From the old farm he and his wife, a textile artist, have converted into a home and studios, there is an impressive panorama. A mountain to the west shields them from the worst storms.

I have become dependent on the ocean and don't think I could bear to permanently lose sight of it. My family has been closely tied to the sea for generations. Both of my grandfathers were captains."

Opdahl doubts that he could paint the way he does anywhere else, for instance, in Oslo where he lived for ten years. That was a critical period of searching, when it was important for Opdahl to be in close contact with other artists.

The coast of Møre is a landscape of shifting moods. The changeable weather and cloud cover can transform it from one moment to the next. Mountains appear and disappear into the fog. It is as though the landscape itself consists merely of light – a light that has substance. Our eyes are pulled toward a glowing patch of sea; before darkness falls, the fog undergoes subtle color changes; in the morning, the milky white sea is tranquil after the night storm. The panorama from Godøy is constantly reborn in a new light, always fascinating.

The artist never turns his back on this landscape, but carries it within himself, as though it were an etching of light which is engraved even in his dreams. When he leaves his workshop – yes, even when he turns out the light at night – his landscape is there. The

moods, the colors, the light never let him go. "I don't believe an artist can help himself; my mind is always painting."

"Norwegians feel a kinship with the land. But we have not always seen the landscape as beautiful. At times we've experienced it mostly as a threat. A boulder might tumble down onto your farm from the mountain, a storm might pull your boat forever below the waves. In our music, our poetry and painting, the landscape is a powerful element which is always present. Even in modern nonfigurative Norwegian art, we can sense the resonance of the Norwegian landscape."

"When the landscape started seeping into my paintings while I lived in Oslo, I felt that I had to fight it. I always put in a figure or two, as an alibi. I simply wasn't ready, either artistically or technically, to just paint landscapes. After all, hundreds of artists have painted western Norway after J.C. Dahl, and it's so easy to get trapped in the landscape of fjords and mountains that tourists see.

Opdahl's mythical dream figures are no longer a mandatory part of his paintings, although the forces of nature seem animated enough. When fleeting figures do reappear, it is as though they are moving through an outer as well as an inner space.

Gradually his painterly effects have become more and more sparse. Opdahl is trying to convey the totality of the landscape, not its infinite details. Yet it is striking how his abstract landscape can at times have an even greater sense of presence than the physical one that surrounds us. Perhaps there is a truth to be uncovered here; when distracting details are peeled away, the essential qualities were made visible, so that they speak more clearly to us. Some of Opdahl's paintings seem almost musical, albeit in the form of a few naked notes that seem to hang forever in the fog, or in the twilight or night which the artist has recreated for us.

The tactile and sensual qualities of Opdahl's paintings allow viewers to feel themselves part of the landscape. His light and shadow are experienced as warmth and coldness. We can feel the jagged rock of mountains against our hands, cleanse ourselves in the cascading light that pours through an opening in the cloud cover, feel ourselves embraced by the dusk and night of his paintings. Opdahl's landscapes are not something we

Ørnulf Opdahl: "Sun and Shadow",
1999. 100 x 100 cm.

watch with an emotional distance. They pull us irrevocably into their atmosphere – an abstract atmosphere which we nevertheless feel physically.

The collective memories that live in all of us, from a history never written down, seem to resurface in some of his paintings. But there is no nostalgia for the past here, no attempt to erase the artifacts of our own age. We glimpse bridges and city lights, burning buildings and oil platforms.

"Western Norway consists of shades of gray, ranging from dazzling white to coal black. This multitude of shades and their orchestration never ceases to fascinate me. If you look closely, you notice that darkness is never black – it always has a color, a temperature. Darkness appears monotonous only at first glance."

"In the catacombs of Rome, where some of the first Christians took refuge for years, someone wrote on the wall almost two thousand years ago: 'In this darkness there is light.' That's quite a statement! I have sometimes

been criticized for making dismally dark paintings. My answer is that in order to paint the light, I have to make room for darkness."

Today, Opdahl uses tempera in virtually all his paintings. He keeps ducks and hens in order to ensure himself a steady supply of albumen. "Tempera is a classical painting technique, but it can also express my own era. I am fascinated by having the freedom to move in two very different directions; I can combine tempera with oil or water, and use almost any painterly medium I want."

He often paints with a varnish. It gives the painting a translucency which allows colors and light to shine through from its depths. Yet he doesn't care for the shiny surface, and so sometimes throws in some sand that he gathers from the beach below the house. The charcoal that Opdahl uses is local, too, dug out from an old Stone Age settlement nearby. "Maybe that is my kind of magic," says Ørnulf Opdahl.

Apples to Tempt Your Senses

Apples from the inner fjord regions of western Norway offer a divine taste – they're one of God's gifts to mankind. A ripe red Gravenstein embraces an entire sunset and reminds you of a blushing lover.

The fresh red color of the peel glows against the white fruit just below; some apples are beautifully marbled with traces of red. When you take a properly large bite, it gives a mouthful at exactly the right moment. Even the consistency is beautiful – not too hard and not too soft. And as it yields it makes the juicy, crunchy sound so satisfying, the sound of nature offering her finest and tastiest treasures to you. Then comes the taste, not too sweet, but with a hint of tartness. Foreign apples usually give a sound of resignation when you take a bite and have a rounder, more anonymous taste.

When Norwegian apples arrive at the grocers, you just have to follow the smell. As if by divine calling, your feet somehow steer you toward the fruit section.

Flowering apple trees

But the apple blossoms of late spring are even more fragrant. When the apple trees unfold their pale flowers toward the end of May, thousands of Norwegians, accompanied by a few early tourists, descend on Hardanger like bees drawn to nectar. Dazzling blossoms of white and pink seduce and overwhelm, and assist the radiant glacier and snow-topped mountains in painting a perfect picture.

Hardanger just wouldn't be the same without blossoming fruit trees. Of course, apple trees are grown other places too. Hjelmeland in Rogaland county, and Leikanger and Hermansverk in Sogn og Fjordane are significant fruit producing districts. The world's northernmost fruit growing area is said to be Valldal on Sunnmøre.

Huge crowns of apple trees rustled by wind and filled with birdsong are only a memory on most fruit farms. The Hardanger poet Olav H. Hauge, himself an apple farmer, tells of how he regretted felling an old apple tree every time he saw the tree stub. He wrote that no apple stored its taste better through the winter than the Flask apples, with "their wonderful spicy taste".

Today, apple orchards look more like vineyards, with tiny trees lined up like soldiers in rows and columns. The trees don't lift their fruit higher than the farmers and their temporary helpers can pluck them all with their feet solidly on the ground.

Other guest workers, too, have to do their tasks. Farmers will rent hives of bees to pollinate their trees. In the autumn we can offer those buzzing insects our thanks as we purchase apples or cherries from one of the youth selling them along the road. Norwegian regulations on insecticides are amongst the strictest in the world. Farmers are forced to get up in the middle of the night, when as few bees and butterflies as possible may suffer harm.

Why are apples from Hardanger so sublime? Their rich taste is the result of fertile soil, long summer days, and the ideal slant of the orchards along the fjord relative to the rays of the sun. There are many sheltered farms along the innermost fjords, and the weather is milder and less rainy than on the coast.

Fragile as eggs

Don't let appearances deceive you – apples are even more fragile than eggs. Harvesting, packing, transport and handling must all be done with the greatest care. One little bruise, even by the shopkeeper, and the apple is soon scarred by a brown blotch just beneath the skin. It takes time, patience and love to give each tree its ideal form. The angle of a branch decides whether it sprouts green leaves, or blossoms soon to be replaced by fruit. Each tree must be pruned and carefully tied, so it will grow the way the experienced farmer wants and yield a rich harvest.

When the summer is hot, farmers are not alone in letting thoughts drift to casks of cool apple cider maturing in their cellars. Perhaps a few apples, too, are stored in a cool place. For many Norwegians, native apples at Christmas have been an important part of the holiday ritual since childhood.

The first seeds

According to tradition, Cistercian monks were the first to plant apple seeds in Norway, probably as early as the 13th century. We do know that Lysekloster monastery, which lies south of Bergen, owned a large farm at Opedal in the Middle Ages. One of the farmers here still has the key to the monastery chapel that once stood nearby. The monks gladly shared their knowledge of nature's growth, and the effect of each herb and other plants on body and spirit. Even though fruit growing gradually spread to other farms in Hardanger, it did not become a major crop before the end of the 18th century – that's when apples and other fruit were carried on sailing ships to cities and towns up and down the coast.

During the 1950s, almost 200 different varieties of apples were sold in Norway. But tough competition and relentless demands for efficiency reduced the number

What youth hasn't been tempted by apple trees with ripe red apples bending the branches low?

to ten or so. Today, the most popular apple varieties are Aroma, Gravenstein and Summerred. New hybrids and varieties are sometimes introduced by apple breeders, but the beautifully marbled Kronprins (Crown Prince), a variety of Prins, arose through natural mutation in Ytre Ålvik in Hardanger. In Ulvik there is now a museum orchard which has saved more than 100 old varieties for posterity. Here, thanks to the Hardanger Folk Museum and the local gardening school, you can purchase apple trees no longer available elsewhere.

The astonished Italians

When Hardanger apples were taken to the annual apple exhibition, Tuttomele ("All About Apples"), in Cavour near Torino, a few years ago, they received much praise. "This is the only place in the whole exhibition where we can really smell apples!" exclaimed the Italians.

Actually, the explanation is simple. In Hardanger, the summer sun shines three hours longer than in northern Italy. Low temperatures let the apples from the west of Norway develop less fructose. On the other hand, they can offer plenty of wonderful aroma and that distinctly tart taste which Norwegian connoisseurs of fine fruit have come to appreciate.

At the end of May, tens of thousands of apple trees burst into bloom and color a scenery second to none.

The Cuisine
of Fjord Norway

The inhabitants of western Norway have long enjoyed the culinary delight of nature's prime food supply. Archeologists have found evidence that oysters and reindeer, for instance, were on the menu in the Stone Age as well.

Cured meats washed down with home-brewed beer – a success with guests for many centuries.

Salmon is tasty served in many ways.

The farms of Fjord Norway are by and large quite small, but that is a sign neither of poverty nor of laziness. Farmers did not require a large plot of the unusually fertile soil to provide well for their families. With few exceptions, the terrain is not conducive to huge farms. For thousands of years, farmers have supplemented their diet with fish – while fishermen have usually grown grains or vegetables. Until modern times, it was common for western Norwegians to eat at least four meals a day.

The list of exotic dishes and ingredients in Norwegian cuisine, however, is not very long; you find most of them in many other countries as well.

Preservation is a key aspect of western Norwegian food traditions. Our predecessors had to store sizable food stocks in order to survive the winter, or when they set sail for distant shores. Both fish and meat were dried, salted or smoked. In addition, some foods were pickled or fermented, or perhaps frozen in the nearby snow or creek. We know that the Vikings used dried and smoked fish as provisions, and that stockfish was actually exported to England a thousand years ago.

Fish

Salt is often the only thing many people will add when preparing fish. The waters of western Norway have an unusually rich sea life. You have to be damned unlucky to return empty-handed from fishing on the fjord or along the coast.

One of the most famous – or infamous – Norwegian dishes is "lutefisk", dried cod which has been soaked in potash lye. It is described in written accounts from other countries in 1540, and thus is probably not originally Norwegian. Some historians have ventured an imaginative explanation of its accidental invention; perhaps a boathouse burned down, so that stockfish was left lying in water and ashes. For many people, "lutefisk" is the culinary high point of Christmas and other festive occasions. There are many ways to serve it – with mustard sauce, goat cheese, or bacon and fat, or mashed split peas.

Both salmon and herring were once common staples, even for poor families. In the 19th century, working class families, too, could afford to buy lobster and oysters. Just like in other countries, the diet was regulated by what was available, but the servants and laborers at large farms would sometimes demand an agreement stipulating that they would not have to eat salmon more than five days a week!

While the Catholics of southern Europe bought imported stockfish from Norway in order to satisfy the commands of Church superiors to abstain from meat at least one day a week, coastal families in Norway looked forward to Sunday dinner when they hoped to set meat on the table.

Meat

No hormones are allowed in Norwegian livestock, nor in imported meat – to the great dismay of the American beef industry.

The sheep of Fjord Norway graze outside for a better part of the year. As a result, the animals are lean and trim, and their natural diet includes herbs that imbue the meat with a fine flavor. But to the trained chef, lamb and sheep that graze on the coastal islands have a very different taste from those sent to pasture on the Hardangervidda mountain plateau.

The native fondness for lamb dishes is perhaps most clearly in evidence at Christmas. Dried mutton steamed over birch sticks are tradition in most families. And any self-respecting teenager learns to make "fårikål" – mutton meat stewed with cabbage and black peppercorns – at an early age. It may take a couple of hours to cook, but preparations hardly take more than ten minutes. If you receive unexpected guests when you're preparing this dinner, you'll be hard pressed to chase them off before mealtime!

Foreign guests, however, are not likely to join in if you serve another time-honored dish: smoked head of lamb. By the time you're through eating, the half cranium before you should be picked utterly clean. It's a feast still appreciated by some modern natives.

The potato

Since the potato was introduced in the mid-18th century, it has been a staple of Norwegian life. Some preachers saw it as virtually a religious duty to spread the good news of this nourishing root. Without herring

There are many variations of "lefser".

Salt meat and potato dumplings is the Thursday special at many restaurants in Fjord Norway.

For centuries, when western Norwegians asked the Lord to grant them their daily bread, they had the all-pervasive crispbread in mind. It was unleavened dough, and baked perhaps only twice a year – but in vast quantities. Crispbread was served at most meals and probably played a key role in the dental care of the region. When the grain crops failed, people would bake bread with ground-up bark; the bark from elm trees was supposed to yield the tastiest bread.

There is a world of difference between the various grades of goat cheese readily available in stores and the tasty home-made product you can buy at some mountain farms. Some connoisseurs of the pungent "gammalost" (literally "old cheese", although it has not actually been aged long at all) give this unappreciated cheese much of the credit for their good health. Modern research on the importance of certain bacteria for our digestive systems may indicate there is some truth to their convictions.

Sugar was once a luxury. As a result, some of the cake recipes inherited by housewives from their great grandmothers may be less sweet than their foreign counterparts.

In the mid-19th century, the temperance movements exerted a strong political influence. Surtaxes and restrictions on sales were enacted, and it became strictly forbidden for people to distill their own hard liquor. As a result, coffee gained popularity as both a stimulant and social drink. Few nations have a higher per capita coffee consumption than Norway. The coffee break is almost tantamount to a sacred ritual; at many offices, the switchboard won't disturb anyone during a coffee break unless the building is on fire!

A toast for moderation!
Today, the Church of Norway is known for promoting a policy of moderation with regard to alcohol. But in the Middle Ages there were actually laws on the books requiring each farmstead to brew ale at Christmas and Easter. Those who refused to abide the law risked having their properties seized – with the King and Church splitting the bounty! (Never mind that the heathen Vikings considered ale and mead one of Odin's greatest gifts to man.)

In some districts, there is also a tradition for making apple cider or excellent wine from dandelion, rhubarb, gooseberries or other fruit.

A new arrival – the fork
More then one Norwegian housewife has been aghast when foreign guests try to cut her cheese with a knife, totally ignorant of the function of the cheese slicer lying in plain view. On the other hand, you can always point out to a Norwegian that the fork only became common in their country as late as 1850.

and potatoes, many Norwegians would not have survived the occasional lean years of the 18th and 19th centuries. Potato dumplings, called "raspeballer" or "komler", often accompany sausages and salted meats and are served with mashed rutabagas.

Bread and porridge
Porridge has provided many of the calories needed by western Norwegians for at least a thousand years. Since it was such a common dish, it was not always appreciated. The saying "Lord, by all means kill me if you wish, but not with porridge!" dates back to the Vikings. Oats or barley were cooked in water, perhaps with milk or cream by those who could afford it. Rice porridge, however, is a more recent introduction, reserved for special occasions in the cities, since it was an expensive import article. Perhaps that is why rice porridge is still a dish associated with Christmas celebrations.

Outermost Reaches of Habitation

Western Norwegians have built their homes in many places we now consider remote, such as on tiny islands with nothing but the Atlantic Ocean and the northern wind as neighbors. God only knows why they didn't seek more sheltered places!

Actually, it's not so strange at all – to some people it made good sense to be near the fishing grounds that provided such a good livelihood. In the face of the awesome sea, people formed closely knit communities and cared less about the distance to town and the mainland.

Ever since Norwegians sowed the first seeds, they have appreciated the fertile soil of the valleys of western Norway. Today, however, agriculture and fisheries are compelled to become evermore efficient, forcing many people to find other means to make a living. Other trades have become more important, and many settlements and villages have actually seen all their sons and daughters move elsewhere.

It's a worthwhile study to take a closer look at the outermost reaches of habitation.

Furthest north in Fjord Norway lies the fishing village of Veidholmen. Today, there are bridges connecting this small group of islets with Smøla and the mainland. Around the harbor of Veidholmen, there are large jetties or breakwaters. In 1936, this was the single most expensive building project that had been carried out in rural Norway to date, and it really was quite complex. The cost of closing off the sounds, pumping the harbor dry, and building the protective breakwaters was exactly

715 229.26 crowns – quite a fortune in those pre-war years! Two years later the locals were grateful, to put it mildly, when a violent storm caused a huge flood wave to crash against Veidholmen. Without the breakwaters, everyone in the fishing village would have been swept to sea, and the old houses that make Veidholmen so picturesque would have been driftwood.

The municipality of Smøla, of which Veidholmen is a part, consists of almost 6000 islands. The people of Veidholmen are still fishing the seas. The local fish processing plant employs 30-40 people.

After Utvær was abandoned to the elements in 1991, at least during the winters, Bulandet inherited the designation as Norway's westernmost outpost. Here, too, 250 islanders live on seven or eight islands linked by bridges. The entire archipelago counts 365 islands – one for every day of the year!

During World War II, Bulandet played a central role in the resistance movement's covert sea traffic to and from the Shetlands. A village museum tells the story of the brave sailors who defied the will and watchful eyes of the German occupants. Bulandet lies northwest of the Sognefjord and southwest of Florø. The modern fish processing plants and the new fishing boats are testimony to the pervasive optimism of the people of Bulandet.

Helgetun is a small group of farms just west of the border to Sør-Trøndelag county. Historians believe that people have lived here for at least a thousand years, although ancient animal pits indicate that hunters found good reason to frequent the area long before that. There are still many deer and moose – as well as very fertile soil. The form of the characteristic houses date back to the Middle Ages. The one-story dwellings could be up to 30 m long and housed several generations. But the farm on the nearby ridge is abandoned.

If you drive several hours southward from Stavanger along the North Sea road, the white houses of Åna-Sira will tell you that you are about to leave western Norway. They bear a closer resemblance to the building style of southern Norway. Actually, the county line, and the river that runs through the village, divide

Åna-Sira in two. A significant number of Åna-Sira's 350 inhabitants work in the shipyards of Flekkefjord, a 20 minute drive further east. A generation ago fishing was the most important source of income for this fishing village; some of the best shrimp trawling grounds in southern Norway were just two or three hours by boat. Today, there are only a couple of fishermen left in Åna-Sira.

Above: The northernmost point
– Veidholmen.

Left page: Bulandet,
Norway's westernmost
year-round habitation.

Right: An abandoned farm
at Rindal, near the easternmost
homes in Fjord Norway.

Bottom right: The village of Åna-Sira lies on
the southern border of Rogaland.

Jæren and Southwestern Norway

The sky above Jæren seems different somehow, unlike that of the rest of Fjord Norway. As you head southward from Stavanger on the North Sea Road, it's easy to imagine that you are moving into a foreign land. When the wind makes billowing patterns in the grain fields, it seems as though golden velvet is being caressed by divine hands.

Norwegian artists are never quite through with the light here, the wide-open fields and the endless pebble and sand beaches of Jæren. Kitty Kielland was the first one who came here to paint. Soon, she was joined by many of her friends, some of the finest artists of their time – Eilif Peterssen, Fritz Thaulow and Harriet Backer. Although, each one had a distinctive style, they can all be considered representatives of the Norwegian National Romantic style. One of the most unusual galleries for contemporary art, by the way, is at Obrestad lighthouse.

Honoring the dead

After the recent Ice Age, Jæren was freed of ice as recently as 14 000 years ago, and hence there has been more time to build up the soil here than in the rest of western Norway. The first people left signs of their hunting eight thousand years ago. Soon they discovered the fertile soil; forests were burned, seeds and root vegetables planted, and in some places the heathlands became the dominant landscape, which was ideal for winter-grazing sheep.

In the course of thousands of years, farmers have cleared the fields of stone. Some have been piled in mile-long stone fences, others carried one by one to make grave mounds for the dead in the Bronze and Iron Ages. There are hundreds of grave mounds in this region, the oldest dating back three thousand years.

Archaeologists have uncovered old settlements and made impressive reconstructions, such as the farm at Ullandhaug. Here, volunteers recreate farm life, crafts and other activities of the Iron Age.

The waves of the restless sea have washed away the footprints and worries of generations of wanderers along the shore. Even when you drive a car along the seaside highway, the ocean can have a healing effect. Along most of the North Sea Road between Stavanger and Kristiansand, which lies near the southernmost part of Norway, you can see the ever-changing sea. The constantly shifting sand dunes, too, are waves restlessly moving onward. In the 19th century, the farmers of Jæren planted marram grass, also known as sea matweed, to bind the dunes so the sand wouldn't blow into their fields.

The wind rarely rests here, even between the tallest dunes. The wind harp that accompanies Jan Garbarek's saxophone on his record "Dis" was recorded at Jæren. The unique instrument was built by Sverre Larssen according to a description in an old Greek legend.

A habitat of birds

When the plows expose the dark, moist earth to daylight, lapwings and other birds have a feast! At the end of the 19th century, before farmers drained many lakes and marshes in order to cultivate more land, bird life here was even more impressive.

Even so, at Lake Grudevatn, more bird species have been observed than almost anywhere else in Norway. Most of the birds who thrive in these wetlands are seabirds and wading birds. Lake Orrevatn is known for its whooper swans; these birds choose partners for life, and

some couples remain here even in the winter. Norway's southernmost bird cliff is Kjørholmane near Sola.

"The land of God's wrath"

Near Ogna, further south, the landscape changes. Sandy beaches give way to an uneven, stony landscape. The road is no longer straight, the curves force you to slow down. Not everyone has been able to see the stark beauty of this barren landscape. The 16th century priest and saga translator, Peder Claussøn Friis, called it "the landscape formed by the wrath of God".

North of Egersund is the huge St. Olav's Serpent, a winding 500 m long moraine that looks more like a huge landscape sculpture. Egersund is the largest fisheries port in the country, at least measured on the basis of catches landed. On the island that shields the town, Eigerøya, stands one of the most powerful lighthouses in northern Europe.

Just before you arrive in Hauge i Dalane, there is a large forest of black alder. If you're up to hiking, the nature conservation area at Rekedal conveys a very special mood. There is a side road that you really shouldn't pass

by – the one that leaves the North Sea Road and takes you to Sogndalsstrand, one of the best preserved shoreside settlements in western Norway. Many of the houses here are from the 18th and 19th centuries.

Do watch the road as you follow the hairpin turns down to the Jøssingfjord – there is not much to protect

Above: Boathouses at Jæren have to be built a safe distance from the shore.

Left page: The retreating ice left boulders in the most surprising places. Some of them are large as houses.

you from the abyss below. Few Norwegian cabins or houses have seen less rain than those huddled under the protective stone overhang of Helleren. Grateful tenants lived here from the Stone Age until the place was abandoned in the 1930s.

Neither ice nor water have made much impression on the hard bedrock in this area. What little soil has been freed lacks nutrients, something that is evident in the sparse vegetation.

Not the quickest road

We'll be honest; the North Sea Highway is not the fastest link between Fjord Norway and Norway's southern coast. But unlike those who travel the inland route of E39, you will arrive invigorated by a fantastic and varied coastal drama. Peder Claussøn Friis was wrong – this landscape south of Jæren is blessed by God, and its beauty will remain with you for a long time.

Above: Kvassheim lighthouse.

Raindrops rarely fall on the rooftops of Helleren!

Egersund has an excellent natural harbor.
In the 1600s, the future town was taking form.

Stavanger –
Harvesting Treasures of the Sea

Some children in Stavanger, and grown-ups too, have an unusual hobby: collecting old labels from sardine cans. No one has a complete set - more than 30 000 different labels have been produced. They are testimony to a prosperous time which brought deep changes to this city.

It must have been a jarring surprise for the locals in 1125, when bishop Reinald arrived from Winchester, England, with a large number of carpenters and stonemasons and announced that he was going to build a cathedral by lake Breiavatn. Stavanger has been a township since that year, but even though it was a center for the imported, Christian faith, which came to dominate all of Europe, for a long time the town as such consisted of a scant group of buildings around the harbor. As recently as 1800, Stavanger had a population of only two thousand.

Except for its decorations, the cathedral has not changed that much. The pulpit from 1658, carved by Andrew Smith, a Scottish master carver, and the large tapestry by Frida Hansen just inside the entrance, showing the coronation of king Olav the Holy, are both worth special notice.

A few generations after bishop Reinald's efforts, Benedictine monks built Utstein monastery, on the northernmost point of Mosterøy island. It is Norway's best preserved monastery.

Three enormous swords appear stuck deeply into the bedrock beside Hafrsfjord, southwest of the city center. They are a monument to Harald Hårfagre and the battle he won here, which united Norway into one kingdom.

Castles for God and people

Stavanger is different from the many European cities that received much of their present form between 1850 and 1950 or so. For the most part, other cities have densely developed city blocks and large buildings of brick or concrete, but as recently as the 1950s, Stavanger was still dominated by small, two-family wooden houses. While the majority of residents in other Norwegian towns were tenants, many more of Stavanger's natives were masters of their own fate, or at least their own "castles".

Prosperous fisheries

The prosperous times began with the rich herring fisheries of the mid-19th century. Soon, a large number of multi-family dwellings had to be built to accommodate the rapidly growing population. Fisheries were incredibly profitable all along the coast of western Norway. Thanks to the "silver of the sea", wealth was soon distributed a bit more equitably. But it was another fish species that led to the growth of the new canning industry – sardines. Canning factories were built along the shore where fishing vessels could more easily unload their catch.

Secondary industries flourished as well – factories that made sardine cans, a rubber industry, shipyards and producers of fishing tackle. Graphic designers and printers started making the first of more than 30 000 labels that adorned the cans.

At one time, fisheries and the canning companies provided a livelihood for 70 percent of Stavanger's workers. The record was set in 1915, when Stavanger produced no less than 350 million cans. As a neutral country during World War I, Norway was able to profit by selling canned goods to both sides.

The world's only canning museum has preserved not only the labels, but a lot of other objects documenting this colorful history. Not until the invention of the refrigerator was there reduced demand for canned fish. There is still a highly specialized canning school in Stavanger.

East and west

Even though almost everyone prospered, clear-cut class divisions remained. A valley passes from the harbor, past Lake Breivatn to Lake Hillevågsvatn. Most of the working classes lived east of this valley, in neighborhoods such as Storhaug.

The schism between west and east, prosperous and poor, seems to be almost a universal phenomenon – and perhaps a deeper analysis could be made of that. In Stavanger, however, the explanation is rather mundane: the wind. The dominant western wind gave most working class neighborhoods a frequent whiff of the penetrating odors from the canning industry. No wonder, then, that those who could afford to lived west of the smelly source.

Old Stavanger

The most fascinating part of the town is Old Stavanger, one of the largest concentrations of wooden buildings in Northern Europe. The old workers' homes, which huddle together along narrow, cobblestone streets, are

Few people would turn down having an address in Old Stavanger. One former tenant was Lars Hertervig, one of Norway's best painters ever.

Old and new meet on the harbor in Stavanger.

almost invariably white. This is not a museum; the residents are grateful locals who can appreciate the charm of this little town within a town.

173 houses from the 18th and 19th centuries have been preserved. Officially, efforts were made to restore this section of town. In truth, the white wooden houses are considerably better kept than when less prosperous residents lived here more than a hundred years ago. Old photographs reveal disrepair of the old, unpainted houses. Through private and publicly financed efforts, the buildings have been "restored" according to our own ideals and aesthetics. In fact, you would be hard pressed to find a single house in all of Stavanger which is authentic as such. But perhaps that is not something to really strive for?

The Oil Age

Many of the old canning factories are still standing, but that's not thanks to any sense of nostalgia. The buildings have very different functions now, some refurbished into apartments, but most of them housing companies involved in other sectors, such as petroleum. At the end of the 1960s, the North Sea once again became the source of prosperity. The great event happened on Christmas Eve 1966 – oil was discovered in the Ekofisk sector. This resulted in hectic activity and further, seemingly chaotic growth in Stavanger. Costly apartment complexes were built in town, and many people could afford to build large houses in the rapidly expanding suburbs.

Many of the platforms that now pump up the "black gold" were built along the Gandsfjord, but the great construction projects here are by and large a completed chapter of our industrial history.

The new literature

The name Stavanger means "the fjord by the steep mountain". We might still call Valberget a mountain of sorts, although it's no great strain to climb the steps to the gallery, café and houses on top.

Many amateur genealogists have received good help from the Norwegian Emigration Center in Stavanger. There are said to be more people of Norwegian descent in the USA than in Norway – of course, that is handily ignoring the fact that they might be 7/8 Irish or 15/16 some other colorful mix.

A statue of Alexander Kielland, the former mayor, overlooks the market place by the harbor. Kielland is better remembered for another contribution; together with Arne Garborg, he wrote some of the first modern Norwegian novels. Even more daring was another literary native son, Sigbjørn Obstfelder, perhaps Norway's first modern poet.

Skudeneshavn

The storms may harry the west coast of Norway, but the old town of Skudeneshavn braves the storms with elegance and style. Skilled craftsmen made sure all the joints were tight on the town's beautiful, Empire style buildings. There are over 125 traditional wooden homes, and 100 boathouses and wharf buildings. The local residents knew how to value their heritage; the houses are well-kept and important details preserved. The original street lights and old-style picket fences fulfill the picture.

This fishing village on the southern tip of the island of Karmøy was settled during the rich herring fishing periods of the 19th century. It is a charming place, sheltered by snaller islands. At its most prosperous time, the locals took over most of the trade from the rich merchants in Bergen and Stavanger. They fished and salted their own catch, and exported it abroad on their own sailing ships. The town had an impressive fleet of trading vessels, especially compared with the number of inhabitants. A number of specialized companies was established as well – one of them exported fog horns to ports throughout Europe.

At the peak of the herring season, there might be as many as 15 000 fishermen in Skudeneshavn. Their heyday lasted from about 1840 until 1870. Every available nook and cranny, even the school and the warehouses, were used to quarter them. In July, when the town is busy with the Skudeneshavn Festival – the many wooden boats in the harbor give an impression of bygone days. Fishing is still very much an active industry.

Skudeneshavn has grown in an "organic" fashion. When Parliament enacted the new Norwegian building regulations of 1854, the local authorities of Skudeneshavn simply claimed that the cliffs and islets "... are obstacles to compliance with the regulations." The main road winds its way, almost path-like, between the white, wooden buildings – no chessboard blocks of streets here. The narrow space between the cliffs and the sea has been cleverly utilized, and there is hardly room for new buildings. Nevertheless the residents of Skudeneshavn lived a life of comfort compared to the often cramped quarters of the working classes in many other Norwegian towns. Most families could even afford to live in a home of their own.

Skudeneshavn enjoys one of the highest average temperatures in Norway. This is evident in the well-cared for gardens and the beautiful park behind the cliffs, established by a women's society who wanted the families and children of Skudeneshavn to be able to share a garden meant for play as well as festive occasions.

Many artists have been drawn to this lively small town and are especially attracted to the special light in this area. Skudeneshavn has a number of galleries. Mælandsgården, an old merchant's house where the interiors are faithfully restored, is now a museum that includes boathouses and workshops displaying traditional tools and old fishing tackle.

They call her "The Lady" – the galleon figure which gazes out over the harbor of Skudeneshavn and back to bygone days. The sailing ships which carried herring to faraway countries are all gone. But this charming, little wooden town still maintains a harmonious character.

Pedestrians and bicyclists need not worry about the rush traffic if they stop for a chat in the middle of the main street in Old Skudeneshavn.

Haugesund –
Town of Many Faces

The confused face of Haugesund is the result of a business boom and certain attitudes that still seem decisive amongst the town's newly rich. We're not talking about the 1980s, when computer wizards and stock market tycoons grabbed considerably more than their share of our common wealth, but rather the 1880s, when the lucrative herring fisheries contributed to a class of newly rich.

Until the end of World War I, buyers in England and on the continent competed for the highest bid for the "silver of the sea", as the herring was called. Enterprising opportunists in Haugesund and elsewhere fished, salted and exported herring like never before. Some of the shipping lines established then still exist, although transporting other goods on distant seas.

What do you do with a new fortune? You build a castle to impress the neighbors, that's what! Show them who you are. The Knutsen villa is a good example of how much one's neighbor means in this respect. Shipping magnate Knutsen's house was originally designed in a Nordic baroque style by architect Ole Landmark in 1895. When a nearby farmer also made a fortune by salting large quantities of herring he erected a copy of Knutsen's villa. The shipping magnate, would have none of that, and immediately gave orders for his own house to be rebuilt!

City of towers

Haugesund is sometimes called "the city of towers". As you walk the streets, you will notice that a sizable number of houses are equipped with corner towers or turrets, or towers that protrude above one of the facades. Some of these "castles" are in the Swiss chalet style, others are Gothic or Neo-Baroque, and still others were built in the Art Nouveau style, albeit with a definite local twist.

Unlike most other Norwegian cities, Haugesund has never been blessed with a large-scale fire to clear the air and provide new building grounds. As a result, we can see how architectural fashions change, one style succeeding another. It is safe to say that Haugesund is a study of contrasts!

The city's unique collection of Classicist apartment and office buildings, Art Nouveau houses of wood as well as brick, white-washed Swiss chalet imitations, and concrete monstrosities from the 1970s and adjacent decades, is all arranged in a strict grid which somehow balances this eclectic mix. Haugesund is structured along two main axes. One extends from the city park in the north to the city hall in the south. The other climbs uphill from the main quay to the town's cathedral.

Farm houses in the center of town!

Astonished visitors sometimes realize they are looking at farm houses in an area otherwise dominated by imposing commercial buildings. It's only a few years ago that sheep were actually grazing on pastures a few hundred meters from the heart of town!

Most of Haugesund's Art Nouveau architecture, which is built of wood, makes less of an imprint on our total image of the city than their sheer numbers would indicate. The reason is the aforementioned contrast, not to say chaos, of styles. In addition, decades of untiring "improvements" have erased many essential details. This, of course, is merely a modernization Haugesund shares with virtually any other Norwegian town.

It was in the years just prior to, and during, World War I that Haugesund developed its own local Art Nouveau dialect. One architect had a decisive influence – Einar Halleland. His faceted towers which decorate many a street corner, and which end in conical roofs, became so imitated that they almost became the local signature of wealth. We won't find similar Art Nouveau buildings in Ålesund, or Swiss chalet-style houses in Stavanger that we might mistake for those here. Einar Halleland, who was schooled in Germany, was one of about fifty architects who contributed to the reconstruction of Ålesund; he designed twelve of the 400 houses erected atop the fire rubble.

If you approach Haugesund by sea from the north, you can't avoid noticing Halleland's largest facade – the Staale building.

A good sense of details

Halleland did not, however, settle for designing facades, making floor plans and construction drawings. When he was put in charge of the new cathedral, he insisted on giving his imprint to everything from door mountings to church benches! He visited the building site regularly, so strongly influencing the master builders that you find echoes of his ideas in their subsequent work. In fact, some of the buildings we might think should be credited to Halleland are actually designed by H.O. Steensnes, a master builder who was not schooled as an architect, but who built quite sophisticated Art Nouveau buildings.

A smith and his apprentice demonstrate their craft during the Harbor Days in Haugesund.

The bridge to Risøy with the harbor in the foreground.

Bergen –
Our Secret Capital

For centuries, Norway's secret capital has faced the ocean and been oriented toward the rest of Europe. Not until the 24th of November, 1909, did Bergen receive a railway link to eastern Norway and Oslo, which is still considered remote and peripheral in many respects. It took even longer before people could drive and not have to stop at a ferry crossing. Bergeners are a breed apart. It's more than a standing joke when they say "I'm not Norwegian, I am a Bergener!"

Bergen means "the meadow between the mountains". Seen from the mountains above, Bergen seems to consist mainly of a promontory and a harbor, and of houses climbing the hillsides. Ulriken is the highest of the seven mountains surrounding Bergen. In decreasing order, the list includes Rundemannen, Løvstakken, Fløyen, Lyderhorn and Damsgårdsfjell. But local patriots are still arguing as to whether Askøyfjell or Sandviksfjell is the seventh peak on the list. Bergen is also surrounded by seven fjords – the Lysefjord and Fanafjord to the south, Raunefjord and Grimstadfjord to the west, the Byfjord and Salhusfjord to the north, and Sørfjord to the east. Seven is a lucky number; it has certainly placed Bergen in a class by itself.

Creativity or endless discussions

Bergen is formed by a strange interplay of two prime characteristics of Bergeners – their creativity, and their endless bickering as to what is the best solution. In 1898, Edvard Grieg himself had to face the most outrageous insults and accusations when he wanted to invite the Concertgebouw orchestra from Amsterdam to a planned music festival. The Bergen Festival has since become an annual event, and the concert hall which bears his name is the main musical venue for the festival.

Plans to upgrade the main square gave rise to heated discussions as well. The solution that received the majority vote is spartan to say the least. The Brancusi-like columns added by Bård Breivik were derisively called "Barbie legs" by detractors. The artist's granite was quarried near the Iddefjord in eastern Norway, where Gustav Vigeland got much of his stone. Breivik received expert help from Chinese craftsmen, most of

them women, when he gave each column its individual form. Heated stone benches provide a dry place to sit just minutes after the rain stops puring. Today, the main square is everyone's meeting place.

Never mind all the talk of what Norwegians are supposed to look like – the native of Norway's most international city is a colorful mix. Besides, the names of the staunchest families reveal the extent of the immigration – Rieber, Mowinckel, Mohn. And judging from their hot-headed tempers, many Bergeners seem to have quite a bit of Mediterranean blood as well.

There is also a monument to Norway's centuries of seafarers on the plaza, made by Dyre Vaa in the 1950s. War sailors and their allies fought a bitter battle to prevent it from being "banished" to the harbor. But perhaps worst of all, in the opinion of self-appointed art critics, was the notion of building an abstract monument to Olav Kyrre, who founded Bergen in 1070. The sheet-metal sculpture is finally in place on a

lawn near the library. Connoisseurs of modern art, too, are disappointed; some believe that the first masterful proposal has been ruined by more than 25 years of committee work.

Everyone, however, agrees that Bergen has perhaps the most beautiful approach by sea of any city in the world. The oldest parts of Bergen are centered around the harbor. The pride of Bergen is "Statsraad Lehmkuhl", a three-masted barque which has many sponsors and supporters. Special bread is baked and sold in the supermarkets of Bergen to raise money for the 98 m long sailing vessel. But the most loyal and humble vessel of Bergen is the tiny shuttle boat which still transports people back and forth between Bryggen and the promontory of Nordnes.

Bergen is a European city of culture – and not just in the year 2000. That is why it seems most fitting that much of Bryggen, as well as the old sardine factory at Verftet, is now occupied by artists and craftsmen,

Above: Mount Ulriken is the highest of Bergen's seven mountains. offering the grandest view of Bergen and her surroundings. On a clear day, the panorama spans from Mount Hornelen at the entrance of the Sognefjord in the north, to Mount Kattenakken near the outlet of the Hardangerfjord in the south!

Left: The Blue Stone, a reclining "monolith" by the city square, is often used as a meeting point for Bergeners.

Bottom left: You may be astonished at how many languages the fish mongers master at Bergen's famous Fish Market!

fashion designers and movie buffs, and those who just want to watch the play of light on the waves while enjoying a cool pint.

Tourists are flabbergasted at how may languages the helpful fish mongers at the Fish Market manage to speak when they see an opportunity to make a sale. Here you can pick saithe and cod right from the tank, fresh shrimp, lobster and smoked eel. In season, there is a good selection of produce from local farmers, and flowers in all the colors of the rainbow.

Right to the church door
The oldest preserved building in Bergen is the Church of St. Mary, probably built at the end of the 11th century. The seashore was much closer then, and people could moor their boats almost right below the church door. After the Hanseatic League established an office in Bergen in 1360, they adopted Saint Mary's as their church. Soon it was richly furnished; there is a magnificent 15h century triptych dedicated to the Virgin Mary, and a beautiful baroque pulpit.

Bergen was the capital of Norway for part of the Middle Ages. At the beginning of the 12th century, the king moved his administration from Alrekstad to Holmen, where Bergenhus fortress stands today. A huge hall was raised by king Håkon Håkonsson in the middle of the 13th century. Håkonshall is still Bergen's most prestigious venue for entertaining guests of high stature. It was heavily damaged when a munitions ship exploded in the harbor on Hitler's birthday in 1944, but it has since been restored.

Rosentkrantz tower was raised during the reign of king Magnus Lagabøte, takes his name from a local lord who reinforced the fortress in the 1560s. It's well worth exploring from basement to roof, and there is a fascinating weapons collection displayed here.

Sailors and kings
American sailors aren't the only ones who have met their great love at Bryggen. This is where Christian II met Dyveke, the commoner who enchanted him and became his very publicly visible mistress. Even when the king was compelled to marry the sister of Karl V, he refused to send Dyveke away. And he was grief-stricken when she later was murdered. Dyveke's mother, a Dutch immigrant, was a trusted counselor and essentially the finance minister to king Christian II.

What do you need to form a town center? A church, a town council, a market place, and a suitable number of inns. For several centuries all this was concentrated at Nikolaikirkealmenningen, which stretched from Bryggen up to Steinkjelleren, at that time the only road to Sandviken. Many of the oldest houses here have a stone or two from the old church that once stood here in their foundations, an ancient custom meant to ensu-

re the Lord's blessing for those who lived there.

One of the main attractions for some Bergeners in the 19th century was located at Stølegaten 11. This was a huge tank of waste beer from the local brewery, freely available and so plentiful that it was called "The Atlantic Ocean".

A view with a coin?
Fløyien is merely a couple of hundred meters' walk and an eight minute funicular ride from the Fish Market. If you continue beyond the souvenir kiosk, restaurant and the metered telescopes, you can climb the higher peaks beyond or even walk across the plateau up to Mount Ulriken.

On a clear day, you can see an astonishingly large part of western Norway from the summit of Mount Ulriken, from the Hardangerfjord in the south to the Sognefjord in the north, with islands and ocean to the west, and the Folgefonna glacier to the east. And the telescopes here don't demand a single coin!

One of Bergen's premier cultural institutions is Fjellveien – the Mountain Road – established by visionary Bergeners headed by Ole Irgens at the end of the 19th century. It hugs the mountain above Bergen, partly shaded by majestic trees, inviting everyone on a comfortable hour-long walk from Kalfaret to Christineplass.

Green spaces
There are generous green spaces in town, too. At Nordnes, the natives stake out their spot in the sun when the clouds thin and the temperature rises. Nygårdsparken, perhaps one of the most beautiful parks in Northern Europe, consists of broken terrain and large, mature trees. At the top of the ridge near the park lies Bergen University – or at least most of it. There is a popular promenade in the park that surrounds the central lake, but everyone pauses when the cherry trees blossom and tulips of many colors unfold. Along the western side of the lake lies an impressive concentration of art museums, with collections spanning from J.C. Dahl and Nikolai Astrup, to Edvard Munch and modern masters.

Height restrictions in Bergen town center were strictly enforced – until city officials elected to build a new town council, a conspicuous concrete tower. Some critics would have preferred that the politicians dug below ground level when they built!

Battle of the cobblestone
In the 1990s, hundreds of thousands of cobblestones once again received a place of honor on city streets. In the dark of night, however, the road authority has actually poured asphalt on some of the most uneven streets, provoking gratitude as well as loud accusations of vandalism. Some drivers merely consider cobblestones a

Gallery owner Reidar Osen used six years to form the unusual interiors of Galleri Nygaten before opening it to the public in 1996 - and his creative work continues.

Bergen offers you a colorful range of cafés.

What harbor in the world bids seafarers a more beautiful welcome than Bergen?

bumpy nuisance. Actually the problem is the old foundation below the cobbles, which was hardly intended for modern lorries and buses.

Without controversy – for once

The wide avenue below Fløibanen is a fine example of the refurbishment of Bergen which has taken place in recent years. Key elements are linden trees and other greenery, cosy benches and beautiful stonework.

Old Bergen has a collection of houses that are carefully placed to give an impression of what the city looked like a handful of generations ago. It may be just as worthwhile to wander in well-kept areas such as Skuteviken, Skansen and Ladegården – and Nordnes, of

course. Much of Bergen has been thoroughly restored and upgraded in recent decades.

Marching to the same drummer

No one can accuse Bergeners of insisting on marching to the same drummer – a fact that makes the drumming youth corps seem like even more of an idiosyncrasy. Carrying swords and make-believe crossbows, and putting on a serious air, they often have an escort of older men and kids not quite old enough to join. Until recently, boys had a monopoly on this kind of ruckus. They may be relatively silent in the winter – but count on it, they're just as sure to reappear in the spring as the white anemones on the hillsides above Bergen. And

At times, in the past, there have been so many boats in the harbor that people could walk dry-shod from one side to the other.
Knud Knudsen, The Photo Collection, University of Bergen.

without fail, the newspapers of Bergen receive a letter to the editor complaining about the noisy disturbances. The letter writer, who often is from Oslo, is firmly told to pack his things and head home over the mountains.

But no one can deny the charm of these street performances. In what other European cities could juvenile gangs march in the middle of the street, slowing down traffic to a snail's pace and trying the patience of scores of drivers, without endangering their very lives! The fact of the matter is that these marching corps offer first as well as tenth generation Bergeners a social focus, and an activity which seems to have done a world of good.

Rhododendron, rain and sunlight

The people of Bergen can be overwhelmingly generous. One businessman gave the city tens of thousands of rhododendrons, which now decorate the thoroughfares into town. Bergen is becoming the undisputed "city of rhododendrons". The robust, leafy evergreen only seems to suffer from lengthy periods of frost or overexcessive sunny spells.

Not to worry! According to meteorologists, there is an average of 200 days of precipitation per year. Even so, the tourism trade was hardly delighted when the local power company started marketing Bergen as "the rainy city". Visitors as well as natives have a strange ability, however, to forget that it may have rained for two weeks straight as soon as the sun breaks through the clouds.

From Rosegrend, one of the best preserved areas of Sandviken.

Lærdalsøyri is one of the best preserved villages in all of western Norway.

Lærdalsøyri

Norway suffered from hectic building activity during the 1960s and 1970s. Aesthetically, the results leave much to be desired. Instead of tearing down their old buildings, the people of Lærdal established a new town center, which could grow at its own new pace.

The oldest wooden houses in Lærdal are from the latter part of the 18th century, but the dominant features are the French Empire and Swiss chalet style of the 19th centuries. The façades are embellished with carved moldings and other elegant detailing. You might get the impression that this is a museum, but Lærdalsøyri is very much alive on its own terms; all but a few of the houses are used year round.

In 1850 Lærdalsøyri was, believe it or not, the largest village in Sogn og Fjordane. Along the fjord, there were 43 boat houses and 15 larger shoreside buildings. During the annual market, which dates back to the 16th century, the farmers would earn good money by renting them out to traders from Bergen and coastal fishermen. The buildings that are still standing are well preserved, not least of all the one they call "The Lieutenant's Wharf".

Long before the experts at the Directorate of Cultural Heritage made recommendations, a committee of local enthusiasts made sure that the unique environment of buildings at Lærdalsøyri was preserved.

Not everyone was pleased when the Directorate placed 170 buildings on a special list to be protected for posterity. "We're not even allowed to paint our houses the color we want," sighed one elderly gentleman. Years later, he and the rest of his compatriots are grateful that Lærdalsøyri's soul and peaceful mood is fully intact.

The queen of Norwegian salmon rivers flows tranquilly through the center of Lærdalsøyri. For almost 200 years, this river has attracted kings and lords, and anglers from other walks of life. It was here King Harald V caught his first salmon, when he was fifteen years old.

Florø

The citizens of Florø have taken good care of their town; in the center, there are many characteristic houses from the latter half of the 19th century and the early decades of the 20th. Most of them have now been equipped with informative signs. This small coastal town was established in 1860, in the midst of the rich herring fisheries.

The Sogn og Fjordane Coastal Museum in Florø has a large collection of objects that illustrate this and other chapters of our cultural history. The pride of their boat collection is S.S. Svanhild, an old ketch which still sails local waters.

There have been only a few brief stretches when Haugesund, a rivaling herring town in the county of Rogaland, has usurped the Guinness record from Florø. True to their nature, the natives of Florø do not enjoy their herring buffet in silence – concerts or Irish music and outdoor dramas have become tradition. Although fishing has always been excellent in the seas near Florø, you hardly have to leave the center of town to make a good catch; the local anglers' association has made sure the central lake is well-stocked for anyone who cares to cast a hook.

The petroglyphs at Ausevik are clear evidence that people have enjoyed the rich natural resources of the area for at least 5000 years. In addition to deer, apparently the most important animal to the artists who created the 300 figures, they portrayed hunters and shamans, painted spirals and sun symbols. Researchers believe one of the figures represents a dog.

The church of Kinn

One of Norway's oldest stone churches, from the early 12th century, stands on the island of Kinn, a 25 minute boat ride west of Florø. Certainly no church has a more beautiful setting! The masterfully carved pulpit from approx. 1250, shows Jesus surrounded by angels and the twelve apostles. Today, only 15 souls live year-round on the island of Kinn. Every summer, however, they are joined by thousands of visitors when 150 actors present one of our most popular historical dramas.

The simple Romanesque church displays many similarities to Irish churches of the same period. A close study of the masonry techniques reinforces the theory that Kinn church actually was built by Irish craftsmen. During the restoration in 1911, a thousand year old Celtic cross was found under the floor boards of the church. According to old legends, one of the boats which accompanied the fleeing Irish princess, Saint Sunniva, shipwrecked on Kinn.

On Svanøy, a picturesque island south of Florø, there is a stone cross supposedly erected by Norway's own saint – Olav the Holy. More striking to most visitors, however, is Svanøy manor, which dates back to 1658.

Førde

The little town at the mouth of the Jølstra river, is host to one of Norway's most colorful music festivals. In early July, audiences are enthralled by the rhythms and melodies of folk music from all over the world.

Førde International Folk Music Festival has been an annual event since 1990 – seven years before Førde gained status as a "town". Førde is a cultural center for the county of Sogn and Fjordane the rest of the year as well, with a well-reputed theater, galleries, and Sunnfjord Museum. This open air museum features fine examples of building traditions dating back to the 16th century.

Agriculture is still the mainstay of this town located on the innermost shores of the Førdefjord, even though a shipyard has been established and there are many other ways to make a livelihood. Førde is surprisingly green, and there is plenty of room between the new houses that gradually creep up the hillsides overlooking the river valley.

According to the Norwegian Bureau of Statistics, the shopkeepers of Førde have the highest per capita turnover of any municipality in Norway. People come from all over the region to make a good bargain, as Førde forms a natural junction between north and south, east and west.

But if your destination is Førde, you better study the map closely; there are four other places in Sogn og Fjordane that bear the same name! There is even a Førde that lies by another Førdefjord – this one a lake.

Førde is located in green surroundings at the mouth of a river, innermost in the Førdefjord.

Ålesund –
the Art Nouveau Town

When Germany's Kaiser Wilhelm II received news of the fire that reduced much of Ålesund to ashes, he immediately ordered four ships to sail north. They were loaded with food and medicine, blankets and building materials originally intended for one of the German colonies. In its time of distress, Ålesund also received aid from other Norwegian towns, especially Bergen, Kristiansund and Trondheim.

It may be hard to believe, but only one person died during the great fire on the 23rd of January 1904. Especially bearing in mind that 800 buildings burned to the ground, and ten thousand people lost their homes! As the prison warden watched the flames approach, he was forced to release his 14 prisoners. He is said to have shouted after them, as they ran for their lives: "Come back tomorrow!"

Rebuilding Ålesund

It took some three years to reconstruct the town, in Art Nouveau architecture but with a definite "Ålesund" interpretation, in which strict geometry is combined with organic forms. These can be seen in the many beautiful details and ornamentation on the buildings – inspired by the National Romantic dragon style, inherited from the Vikings.

The buildings constructed after the fire were all of stone and brick. Corner pieces and ornamentation were often sculpted from natural stone, including granite from the Iddefjorden in Østfold – the quarry used by Gustav Vigeland for his famous monolith in Oslo's Vigeland park. Two streets in the town were widened in order to prevent any future fire from spreading to the old wooden neighborhoods still left standing.

The merchants and businessmen of Ålesund now felt a need to prove that they were modern. Planners emphasized amenities such as running water, electricity and large windows to let in sunlight. Flush toilets were installed, too, whereas the old buildings had such facilities in the back courtyard. But despite what was fashionable elsewhere, many buildings were designed to house both apartments and businesses.

If you wander the streets of Ålesund, you realize that the master glaziers must have had quite a challenge. The great variation in form and size of the windows made it impossible for these craftsmen to save time by mass-producing any of the windows.

Rebuilding the town cost 19 million crowns, but insurance covered only half. Thanks to the prosperous herring fisheries in the years preceding the fire, the property owners also had some funds of their own. And even though the banks no longer considered towns that had fisheries as their prime source of income to be particularly lucrative investments, they lent them the remaining five million.

Hungry architects

At the end of the 19th century, there was a construction bust in the major Norwegian towns. Architects suffered, too. When most of Ålesund had to be rebuilt, many of them packed their drawing boards and headed there, hungry for new work.

Half of the 50 architects that competed for assignments were under 35 years old. Most had attended schools in Germany, others had trained in England or Scotland. But they all shared a vision of building something new – to manifest a dream of what Norwegian architecture was meant to be. They were also well aware of architectural trends on the continent.

Even though they competed with each other, their building designs were variations on a common theme – Art Nouveau, or Jugendstil. The aesthetic unity is striking, especially taking into account that the authorities did not have time to enact a detailed plan regulating the rebuilding of Ålesund.

The architects rebelled against the dominant tendency to mix current styles at will, perhaps adding older element thanks to the misunderstood nostalgia of National Romanticism. Yet the Art Nouveau of Ålesund incorporates both dragon style and Gothic elements.

Architecture and city planning

The best way to see Ålesund and the surrounding panorama is from Aksla – 418 steps take you to the top. Apart from the westernmost part of town, very few wooden buildings from before 1900 remain. From a lower hill where Aalesund Museum is situated, you can better appreciate how the buildings of the town flow with the uneven terrain.

Influential city planners, such as Camillo Sitte of Austria, no longer held the strict grid as their ideal. On the contrary, they believed that an irregular terrain had a charm of its own, and that the placement and direction of streets should be adjusted to it. These city planners were not the only ones fighting against architecture lacking a human dimension or based on exaggerated use of right angles and straight lines.

Perhaps just as decisive a consideration in Ålesund was a lack of time. It hardly seemed right to postpone building, just to flatten out the terrain, when ten thousand people lacked permanent homes.

Industrious the people of Sunnmøre

There are numerous jokes told about the people of Sunnmøre who are known for their enterprise. The well-known author Agnar Mykle is rumored to have claimed that: "You can leave a Sunnmøring on a deserted island out in the middle of the ocean, and if you go back after three months, he'll have managed to start a furniture factory and build a chapel."

One thing is for sure – the construction sites saw buildings rise at a record tempo. Today, Ålesund accounts for three quarters of world klipfish exports, the same market share as before the catastrophic fire.

As the town's population gradually increased, new buildings and land were required. A large part of the town today is actually built on reclaimed land. Even the seagulls had to make way for progress – and today, politicians and bureaucrats nest in the town hall, on top of what was once the town's bird rock.

Down by the harbor, you often see ships moored and being loaded with furniture and dried fish, which is exported all over the world. Fishing and fisheries play a strong role in the history and traditions of Ålesund. Unlike the people of Northern Norway, who hang their cod on drying racks, the people of Sunnmøre lay their catches out to dry on the rocks by the shore. The fishermen of Ålesund have provided many a bowl of bacalao for southern Europeans and South Americans!

The history of Ålesund goes back over 800 years. During the 11th century, a trading post was established

No other port in Europe has such a harmonious concentration of Art Nouveau architecture.

Ålesund looked like a war-ravaged
city after the fire of 1904.
View from Aksla.

Amazingly, Ålesund was rebuilt in
three years, and since then the town
has essentially kept the unity of its
Art Nouveau architecture intact.

near where Sunnmøre Museum and Borgund church
now stand, 4 km east of today's Ålesund. This settlement was abandoned after the plague of 1349,

Architecture with a smile

The Art Nouveau of Ålesund seems to possess an optimism – it is architecture with a smile! Art Nouveau is
often characterized by an excellent cooperation betwe-
en architects, craftsmen and artists. And factories too –
mass production was often embraced as a means to
provide people with inexpensive products of beautiful
design.

Those who think they see an Asian influence in Art
Nouveau architecture are not imagining things. The
arts and craft of Japan, especially, were an important
inspiration to European art, architecture and industrial
design.

In the 1970s, few people seemed to appreciate the
Art Nouveau buildings of Ålesund, at least judging
from their lack of maintenance. Today, they are everyone's pride and the people of Ålesund consider this
architectural heritage as their very own. An Art
Nouveau center – Jugendsenteret – has been established
in a particularly beautiful stone building, were the
interiors are still intact. Many of the buildings erected
after the fire are now protected. When developers wanted to demolish five Art Nouveau buildings in 1997,
there was so much resistance that three of them were
spared.

There are other European cities with a visible infu-
sion of Art Nouveau, among them Glasgow, Brussels,
Nancy, Vienna, Barcelona, Terassa, Riga, Budapest and
Ljubljana. But nowhere else do you find the concentration which creates the harmonic whole that places Ålesund in a class by itself. It should come as no surprise
that Ålesund is a strong candidate for UNESCO's World
Heritage List.

Molde – the Smell of Roses, the Rhythm of Jazz

Molde is fragrant roses, the rhythm of jazz, a panorama of snow-clad peaks, and the satisfied smile of people going about their tasks or perhaps stopping to breathe deeply of life during a moment's pause.

It hasn't always been thus – it was deathly quiet after German bombers reduced two thirds of the city to rubble in April 1940. Molde suffered two weeks of intense bombing against civilian targets, even with fire bombs. The Allies landed troops that tried to hinder the advance of German ground forces, but without success. The last impression King Haakon and Crown Prince Olav had as HMS Glasgow sailed out from Molde harbor, was of fire consuming the church and its tower tumbling into the flames. The royal family was evacuated together with the Norwegian government, a large corps of diplomats, and the gold stores of the Bank of Norway.

Putting Molde on the map

I'm afraid we're skipping some essential chapters of our history. On 16th century Dutch maps, there are 130 place names entered around the Romsdalsfjord. What qualified them was that a new invention was installed there: water-driven sash saws. These saw mills produced materials used to reinforce dikes in the Netherlands, and poles to support the buildings and quays of Amsterdam.

In 1533 the island of Bud, 41 km northeast of Molde, experienced dramatic days. This was where Olav Engelbrektsson, the last archbishop of Norway, tried to gather the Council of the Realm in order to select a new king. Today Bud is a tiny fishing village; in the 16th century it was the largest trading post between Bergen and Trondheim. The archbishop failed in his last attempt to save the influence of the Catholic church in the Dano-Norwegian kingdom. In the next few years the full onslaught of the Reformation swept away the vestiges of Catholicism.

Molde was granted township status in 1742, partially thanks to the prosperous summertime herring fisheries in the nearby fjords. Molde's coat of arms shows a whale chasing the herring right into a barrel – but there was a bit more to it than that!

Present Molde is not noted for its great architecture. The dominant style is a sober post-war functionalism.

The notable exceptions when it comes to good design are the cathedral and city hall, but if we approach Molde from the east, we pass a number of stately mansions dating back to the 18th and 19th centuries.

Roses

Before you point out that you've seen more impressive rose gardens in France or southern England, you should reflect on the fact that Molde is situated even farther north than Anchorage, Alaska. The roses here blossom later than their botanical sisters on the continent, but you can enjoy their flowers longer.

The first roses in Molde grew in the well-kept gardens of the officers of the Crown, where they shared the fragrant company of lilies, lilacs, peonies and honeysuckles. Their efforts were soon imitated by others.

One of the first to mention Molde's beautiful gardens, was a city doctor in 1790. He ascribed the good health of the working classes, who were quite poor, to their admirable ability to create beauty around themselves.

At the end of the 19th century, Molde was one of Norway's premier cruise destinations. Hotel Alexandra was named after the English princess, in line with our seemingly universal tendency to try to flatter those who can provide for our wealth. Soon it was almost to be expected that the directors of the local hotels were waiting with a generous bouquet of roses, selected from the hotel gardens, when a ship cast anchor. Before the turn of the century, Molde was known throughout Europe as "the city of roses". German rose-breeders have even named one of their new cultivars "Molde".

The inspiration of Art

Molde has inspired many creative efforts – among them Henrik Ibsen, Bjørnstjerne Bjørnson and Alexander Kielland. The gloomy, almost misanthropic Ibsen never received the Nobel Prize, while the jovial Bjørnson, who grew up at a vicarage in the neighboring municipality, did. An annual literary festival honors Bjørnson and other Norwegian and international authors.

The challenge of counting mountains

The best place from which to admire the Molde panorama, which counts 222 peaks, is Varden, 406 m above sea level. It's a worthwhile hour-long walk from town, or a briefer drive if you're in a hurry. For those who suspect patriotic Moldensians of exaggerating, someone has taken the trouble of printing a little pamphlet actually listing each of the 222 mountain peaks! Even a brief walk up Rekneshaugen, 70 m and in the center of town, takes you up to an impressive view of 87 mountain tops.

That's not the only thing worth seeing from Rekneshaugen. Romsdal Museum, an outdoor museum that allows you to dwell in the past, not just of Molde but of the surrounding districts, is also here. Efforts have been made to recreate one street as it appeared before the bombs fell. At Hjertøy, an island 10 minutes from the city center, there is a fascinating fisheries museum, a branch of the Romsdal Museum.

Jazz

You could write a credible history of modern jazz by limiting yourself to musicians that have played at Molde International Jazz Festival – Dexter Gordon, Oscar Peterson, Keith Jarrett, Jan Garbarek… Four decades of festival programs would leave few omissions. Quite the contrary. To festival organizers, "jazz" is clearly a very flexible notion; the list also includes Eric Clapton, Ray Charles and Bob Dylan.

Outstanding Moldensians

We suspect that those who built Molde's football stadium of wanting to impress everyone who arrives by sea. One can hardly accuse them of insisting on humble dimensions; the stadium has room for half the city's population! You may be astonished to hear that this monumental venue for sporting events is a gift from millionaires Kjell Inge Røkke and Bjørn Rune Gjelsten, indisputably Molde's best poker players on volatile financial markets.

From the market place in Molde.

Another native son has shown exceptional abilities in the political arena. Despite being made the laughing stock of the establishment and national press when he revealed his ambitions, and despite having the narrowest parliamentary support of any modern prime minister, Kjell Magne Bondevik served as prime minister for 29 months, admirably managing the fine act of balancing the various opposition parties. Bondevik has also proved to be a capable football commentator.

No one who approaches Molde by sea can avoid noticing the huge football stadium, which opened in April 1998. It accommodates half of all Moldensians!

Kristiansund –
City of Merchants

Actually, klipfish was not Kristiansund's first export. During the 17th century, the region was exporting timber – and Jappe himself was originally a timber merchant. He didn't try to claim undue credit for the wind-dried fish, however. He explained that his "Terra Nova fish" was based on drying techniques he had learned in Newfoundland and in the states of New England, where they produced vast quantities of such fish. Even though the king granted Ippes a monopoly on his trade, he went bankrupt after seven years. Fifty years later, British merchants were tempted to come here on similar terms. For many years, Kristiansund was virtually a British colony!

Years of rich fisheries
In 1742, Christian VI gave Kristiansund township status, privileges which the merchants in Bergen and especially Trondheim were against. They felt their economic position threatened. In gratitude to the king, the locals honored him by renaming their town Christiansund. Herring was the most important catch in the 18th century. Spring-spawning herring was caught in closing nets drawn against the shore. Fisheries were particularly good from 1730 to 1750. Then suddenly one year the herring was gone – catches dropped from 75 000 to 2000 tons.

Fortunately, the klipfish trade was really blossoming. Within 1790, the merchants of Kristiansund were selling all the klipfish they managed to produce to foreign markets. Needing more fish, they sent their schooners northward to Lofoten to buy it.

Unlike stockfish, klipfish is skinned and the spine removed, then salted before being dried. As a result, the fish can be stored longer before it being dried. Today it is cliff-dried fish in name only; modern klipfish is dried indoors in special drying tunnels.

Wealthy merchants
By the 19th century, Kristiansund had become one of the most important export ports in Norway, and there was a growing class of wealthy merchants. Some of them were well-traveled and spoke four or five languages. The local dialect still contains Spanish words and audible influences from other countries. Also in other respects, Kristiansund was at the forefront. It was one of the first towns blessed with a new drink – coffee –

as well as exotic foods imported from warmer lands.

In the 1850s, the town of Kristiansund started exporting klipfish directly to South America. A special crate was developed for that purpose. It was lined with soldered tin, which almost provided a complete seal. Tinsmiths were suddenly in dire need. In order to meet demands any way they could, the merchants convinced the king to drop restrictions on this craft. Usually, only craftsmen belonging to the proper guilds were allowed to produce these crates. The boatyards of Kristiansund also built special cargo ships designed for sailing in tropical waters.

In the 1880, Kristiansund experienced an economic crisis. During an international slump in the 1870s, the klipfish merchants decided to grant their foreign buyers credit. It turned out to be a grave mistake; when the market collapsed, Nikolai H. Knudtzon III was the only merchant who managed to stay solvent.

When other trade fleets were switching from sail to steam, Kristiansund lacked the finances to acquire steamships – at least not anywhere near the number of vessels in the sailing fleet of the past. When other Norwegian cities and towns were well on the way to recovering from the depression, Kristiansund was still struggling. Kristiansund had the dubious honor of being the first Norwegian municipality to go bankrupt; the town was placed under public administration in 1920 and again in 1932.

Over the following years, fortunes turned. Kristiansund pioneered the use of ocean trawlers, and could even be called the country's "trawler capital" by 1950. Today, shipbuilding and offshore industries are the town's main sources of income. The Draugen and Åsgård oil fields are located nearby. The shipping industry builds on proud traditions. Mellemværftet, a shipyard established in 1857, which is now part of Nordmøre Museum, is one of the finest when it comes to restoring old vessels.

Three islands
Kristiansund is built on three islands at a junction of fjords. In this day and age, few people reflect on the fact that the city lies 10 km from the mainland. Except for the occasional maintenance job, the same boats have shuttled passengers across the sounds of Kristiansund

The Dutchman, Jappes Ippes, was the first to try to make money by drying fish on the cliffs of Nordmøre. In fact, that's why it's called klipfish. That was the real cornerstone of Kristiansund, on top of 8000 year old settlements.

"The Klipfish Woman" is a monument to everyone who, through the years, has contributed to the lucrative export of klipfish.

These shuttle boats have trafficked
the sounds of Kristiansund
since 1876.

since 1876. They still do, even though bridges enable people to drive across.

By the way, the harbor is the true town center of Kristiansund. You don't really see the fine, natural harbor before you actually sail into it. Kristiansund has once again become a destination for cruise ships, as it was during the interwar period.

The wooden town that vanished

Not many people are aware that the wharf here dates from the 17th century and is 60 years older than the famous Bryggen in Bergen. Unfortunately, commercial interests in Kristiansund did not value this cultural heritage properly; 11 old wharves were torn down in the 13 years preceding the new millennium.

Flames of destruction

If it had not been for certain catastrophic events, Kristiansund might well have consisted of one of Europe's most impressive collections of wooden buildings. At the beginning of the 20th century, the town had a unique selection of architecture from different periods. The reason for the delightful architectural mix, was Kristiansund's long-lasting exposure to varied impulses from abroad.

There are still many houses close to 300 years old. In the part of town called Innlandet, many working class houses and a single patrician home have been preserved. A large part of the area around the harbor, where the Klipfish Museum and Mellemværftet shipyards are located, is intact. The rest of old Kristiansund can be admired only through historical photographs.

No other Norwegian city suffered so heavily from the bombs that fell during the war. Historians are still searching for the reason for the attack; they have not found any orders for the bombing. There were no war ships in the harbor, Kristiansund had no military installations, and there were, at most, a handful of soldiers in the city. The harbor master patrolled Kristiansund with a signaling gun! Almost two thirds of the city's buildings were destroyed in the massive bombing between the 28th of April and the 2nd of May, 1940. It is a miracle that only five people were killed!

Reconstruction

The people of Kristiansund have never sat around waiting for others to do things on their behalf. As soon as they could start rebuilding, they contacted Sverre Pedersen, Norway's foremost city planner at the time. Leading architects such as Arne Korsmo, Jacob Hansen and Erik Rolfsen have helped formed the city, providing it with clean, functionalistic architecture. Perhaps not long from now, these buildings will be more highly appreciated; not many decades ago, Ålesund's Art Nouveau architecture received only words of derision.

In 1992, Kristiansund was linked to the mainland through Krifast, a road project that included the hundred-meter-high Gjemnessundet bridge and the 5.1 km long undersea tunnel to Frei, an island south of Kristiansund.

In Spanish earth

Kristiansund has a long tradition of burying her deceased sons and daughters in Spanish earth, a local custom which requires an explanation! When vessels returned after delivering cargoes of klipfish in Spain, they unloaded soil that had been used for ballast – some of which was used in one of the local cemeteries.

The opera

Considering her strong, continental bonds, it's not so strange that Kristiansund was the first Norwegian town to establish an opera – long before our capital did. At the beginning of the 19th century, the merchants of Kristiansund would organize concerts for each other's enjoyment.

Traditions have continued, except that today's cultural events bid everyone welcome. The central venue of the annual Opera Festival, held in February, is a grandiose Art Nouveau building erected in 1914. Another Art Nouveau building that survived the bombs was Nordlandet church, built in local granite the same year. This church has beautiful stained glassed windows designed by Emanuel Vigeland.

Pigeons in courtship

Architectonically, the church designed by Odd Østbye, who won the design contest for Kirkelandet, is certainly the most interesting of the town's churches. A few days before the deadline, he had a set of drawings ready to submit. Then he saw two pigeons engaged in courtship in a central square in Oslo. With renewed inspiration, Østbye frantically drew night and day and won the contest.

It is surprising that there was hardly any resistance to Østbye's radical design. The natives of Kristiansund argued, all right, but only about the placement of their church. The team of architects in charge of rebuilding the town felt reason for disappointment. The integrated plan they had envisioned, with an axis from the harbor up to the church, and with a cultural market at the top of the hill forming the heart of the city, was ignored. Instead, Kristiansund received a large bank at the top of the hill. But maybe that, too, is a monument of sorts?

Locals sometimes refer to Odd Østby's unusual church as the Atlantic Cathedral. Everyone who enters the church is affected by the lights and the strong play of lines.

The altar of Grip stave church, which dates back to 1520, was a gift from a Dutch princess.

Sources and assistance:

This book could not have been written without the help of many experts who have graciously shared their knowledge and insights with us:

Thor W. Bjørlo, Nils Georg Brekke, Karl Egil Buch, Oddmund Fjøynes, Alv Ottar Folkestad, Ågot Gammersvik, Julie Hansen, Øystein Jansen, Oddvar Johan Jensen, Emil Kaland, Johannes Kleppa, Mons Kvamme, Hans Emil Linden, Anne Kristin Mikalsen, Nils Nonås, Kristin Norseth, Henry Notaker, Jenny Rita Næss, Ørnulf Opdahl, Tone Rasch, Erik Solheim, Ola Storsletten, Randi Sunde, Sverre Johan Svendsen, Berit Kvinge Tjøme, Marco Trebbi, Vidar Tøsse, Marit Synnøve Vea, Olav Vinddal and Signe Aarhus.

In addition, many museums and other cultural institutions, as well as adventure centers, have provided valuable assistance. We would especially like to thank:

Edvard Grieg Museum Troldhaugen, the Hanseatic Museum, Art Nouveau Center (Jugendsenteret), Hardanger Folk Museum, Nordfjord Diving Service, Norwegian Bunad Council (Norsk Bunadsråd), and Strømsholmen Sea Sport Center.

The most important written sources have been:

Brekke, N.G. (ed.). 1993. Kulturhistorisk vegbok Hordaland. Nord 4 Vestkyst.
Graham-Campbell, G. 1982. Vikingenes verden. Tiden Norsk Forlag.
Hartvedt, G.H. 1999. Bergen byleksikon. Kunnskapsforlaget.
NAF Veibok 98. Evensen, K. (ed.).
Notaker, H. 1996. Ganens makt – Norsk kokekunst og matkultur gjennom tusen år. H. Aschehoug & Co.
Notaker, H. 2000. Biografi over norske kokebøker, Nasjonalbiblioteket
Olderkjær, O. 1982. Norske fyr. Samlaget.
Solheim, E. 1999. Jostedalsbreen – vandringar i nasjonalparken. Nord 4. Storsletten, O. 1993. En arv i tre – de norske stavkirkene. H. Aschehoug & Co.

In addition, we have used an extensive background literature and secondary sources.

Other photographers:

Lynx p.38 Johannes Jensås
Stag deer p.41 Øivind Leren
Eagle p.42 Johannes Jensås
Oyster catcher p.43 Johannes Jensås
A Cradle of the Industrial Revolution p.92–93 The Knud Knudsen Collection, Norwegian Industrial and Hydropower Museum
The Story of the Bergen Railway p.100–101 Knud Knudsen, The Photo Collection, University of Bergen
A Bicycle Adventure on the Mountain Plateau p.102–103 Egil Korsnes
The Hardanger Fiddle p.106–107 Egil Korsnes
"Bridal Voyage in Hardanger», Adolph Tidemand & Hans Fredrik Gude p.109 Courtesy of the National Gallery
Goats p.122 Johannes Jensås
Rauma ullvarefabrikk s. 111 Lars Kristian Crone
The Troll oil platform, Climbing maintenance worker p.126 Courtesy of Statoil
Downhill skier p.129 © Edelpix, Jeff Webb
Salmon fisherman p.132 Øivind Leren
Molde International Jazz Festival p.136 Ulf Johanessen
Portrait of Edvard Grieg p.144 Courtesy of Edvard Grieg Museum Troldhaugen
Portrait of Fartein Valen p.145 Courtesy, Lyche Forlag
"Motif from Borgøy», Lars Hertervig p.147 Courtesy of the National Gallery
"Midsummer Eve Bonfire», Nikolai Astrup p.148 Courtesy of the National Gallery
"From Stalheim», J.C. Dahl p.149 Courtesy of the National Gallery
Apples p.152 Johannes Jensås
View of Bergen from Mount Ulriken p.173 Willy Haraldsen
Ålesund after the fire p.184 Courtesy of Sunnmøre Museum
Molde p.186–188 Øivind Leren
Kristiansund p.189–191 Ivar Halvorsen

Publisher:

KOM Forlag a/s
www.komforlag.no
post@komforlag.no

Author: nextchap@bgnett.no (Olav Grinde)

Photographer: pereid@online.no (Per Eide) www.pereide.no
Co-author: Linda Renate Campbell
English consultant: Melody Favish

© KOM Forlag
Project coordinator: Svein Gran

Graphic design: Lillyputt/Kanon
Printed by PDC Tangen 2004

ISBN 82 90823 59 2 (English edition)
ISBN 82 90823 58 4 (Norwegian edition)